TABLE OF CONTENTS

OPERATIONAL STRATEGY   127

FINANCIAL STRATEGY   143

INTRODUCTION

We were sailing in the middle of the Adriatic Sea, halfway between Italy and Croatia, more than 75 nautical miles from any land, with our whole family on our sailboat, Dragonsinger. At our average speed it would take us ten hours to reach land. We were in our third night on passage when we spotted a thunderstorm as wide as the horizon. Karalee and our daughter Jocelyn got me up at midnight to ask me what to do about the storm. I said to leave it to port (the left side of the boat) and went back to bed to get more rest.

At 0200, my ten-year-old son Kevin and I got up to take our three-hour watch. Lightening struck the water in front of us every minute or two. We continued sailing towards the storm for an hour. With the lives of our family at stake, I finally told Kevin we needed to "heave to." This sailing maneuver quieted the motion on board while stopping Dragonsinger in its tracks pointing the stern of our boat towards the storm.

For an hour, Kevin and I watched the storm. Every fifteen minutes, we got up, took a 360-degree look around the horizon, and checked the radar for other boats and to see if the storm was getting closer. After an hour of careful observation, we concluded that the storm was moving very slowly from left-to-right. If we had continued on our port tack, we would have ended up right in the middle of the thunderstorm. We tacked the boat onto starboard and left the storm to our right-hand side, continuing safely through the night.

The lesson from this is that even when the stakes are as high as they can be (with the lives of my family at stake), the correct course of action was to stop what we were doing, evaluate, and then proceed. Working on a strategy for your business takes the same kind of discipline:

> Slow Down to Speed Up

ACCELERATE NOW

My goal is for you to step into action to accelerate your business today. I promise that if you slow down and spend one hour reading *Wind In Your Sails*, you will have three ideas that will accelerate your business in the next 90 days.

ENTREPRENEURS

I am a successful entrepreneur who has experienced the ups and downs of running my own business. Use my experiences to inspire you to think about and operate your business in new ways, while avoiding some of the pitfalls I, and the entrepreneurs I discussed in this book, learned the hard way.

Many books explain theories of leadership, strategy, marketing, or sales. This book gives you all of that plus outlines the concrete actions you can take now to create sustainable change so your business prospers. Learn firsthand about the real-life challenges that I and ten other entrepreneurs have faced and how we overcame them to be successful.

FIND YOUR ANSWERS

There is no single answer for how to successfully market and sell your products or build your business. There are ways to manage your strategic approach and tactics, and methods for how you measure and motivate your employees that can have a massive impact on your business results.

If you are feeling stuck, the answers are here. This book combines my thirty-five years of entrepreneurial experience with the hundreds of years of combined experience shared by the entrepreneurs I interviewed to provide you with proven ways to succeed. I know that this book will get you to think and act differently today. The proof will be in the ways your business accelerates in the next 90 days.

PUTTING IT TOGETHER

I have presented the information in this book in a way that I think any entrepreneur can benefit from. Each chapter is self-contained, so if you work better by jumping into the middle, feel free to read the book that way. The book is organized into the ten strategic areas of every business. The areas are:

TEN STRATEGIES:

Entrepreneur
Corporate
Innovation
Marketing
Sales
Product
People
Operational
Financial
Exit

Entrepreneur: As an entrepreneur, you have the biggest impact on your business. Your personal growth, how you show up, and the ways you lead ultimately determine the success of your business and your life.

Corporate: A strategic plan outlines your ten-year vision. Strong plans then have concrete goals for the next three years, one year, and next quarter. High growth businesses commit to corporate strategic planning by getting off site once a quarter.

Innovation: In today's world all businesses have to innovate. Innovation isn't just about technology; it is as much about how you innovate in all of your processes and the approach you take to markets and people.

Marketing: Businesses that perform well put time and energy into understanding their markets, the key characteristics of their customers, and the critical things that make your company and your products different from those of your competitors. They then tie this into all the activities and communication channels that apply to their markets.

Sales: Predicting revenue requires that you have a proven sales process. Successful sales leaders use key measures from their sales process to monitor activities in real-time. Innovating and being creative in your approach to sales channels will give you a competitive advantage.

Product: Whether you sell a physical product, a service, or a promise, there are product strategies that can dramatically improve your sales and the success your customer's have with your product. Combining market knowledge, innovation, and product strategy lets you lead your market—if that is what you want to do.

People: People buy products and services. People deliver them. People create products. The success of your business is tied directly to how well you attract, retain, and motivate the people in your business.

Operational: Highly successful brands make a marketing promise that the brand delivers over and over again. Learn how to create a Promise Delivery System that lets you measure and deliver on your brand promise day after day.

Financial: Entrepreneurs create a business to solve a market need they identify. Few have financial training, yet the strategic management of your finances, from raising capital to managing your cash flow, can have an enormous impact on your bottom line.

Exit: To maximize your return when selling your business, start with the end in mind. Whether you plan to sell next year or in ten years, there is a process and method to thinking about your exit strategy that ensures you will be successful when you are ready to exit the business.

GET GOING

Every chapter includes a case study demonstrating the strategy for the chapter and three action challenges you can take to help you move up a level in your thinking and actions for your success. Learning and thinking are fabulous, but action is what produces results. Jump in now. I challenge you to read a chapter in the next hour and create three specific tasks that you will take to accelerate your business in the next 90 days.

What Are You Waiting For?

ENTREPRENEUR STRATEGY

It was 1980 and I had just graduated with a degree in Computer Science from the University of British Columbia. I had been working for about seven months. Bob Green, who had hired me, and I agreed that even though I had three years of commercial programming experience I still needed to gain more. Bob arranged for me to work as a consultant to the Bentall Group, one of the largest land developers in Vancouver. I worked on the 36th floor of their iconic Bentall Tower III, at the time one of the largest office towers in Vancouver and still a landmark today.

After completing my degree, I knew I needed a break. The previous summer, I had purchased my first boat. The plan was that Karalee and I would take four weeks to sail up and down British Columbia's west coast. I started at the Bentall Group in May and no one was very enthusiastic about my taking four weeks off in the summer, but I knew it was the right thing for me to do.

In that first year at the Bentall Group, I wrote 100,000 lines of production COBOL code., compared to the industry average of ten lines of code per day or approximately 2,500 lines per year. As a junior programmer, the designs were set, reports were straightforward, and I could have probably done even more if I had used one of the 4th generation reporting tools that were then becoming available. While many questioned my decision to take so much time off, the truth was that I needed the break to recharge myself. The proof was in the productivity I was able to demonstrate in that first year after returning from our sailing holiday.

LEADERS SET THE TONE

As the leader of your organization what you say and do is amplified a hundredfold. If you are having a bad day, your body language will reflect it, and the staff will assume that the company is having a bad day. Make yourself accountable and your employees will hold themselves to a high standard. Every day you set the tone for the business.

Most of us show up at work with our default behaviors. Have courage, look at how you are acting and behaving, and then decide if that is the tone you want to set for your business. Powerful changes can happen when you take personal leadership to a new level.

You will be challenged when you make a decision to show up differently every day. To start, just act "as if" you had already made the change to a new way of doing things. You will inevitably fall back into old habits from time to time. When you catch yourself, go back to acting "as if" you had already arrived at your new way of doing things. If in doubt, seek out feedback on how you are doing from those closest to you. You decide what your tone will be—the rest of the company will follow.

LISTENING

I like to talk. Often I like to talk a lot. To truly communicate, you need to build your listening skills far more than your speaking skills. Cultivate great listening skills by focusing on:

Speak Less: Nature gave us two ears and one mouth so that we can listen twice as much as we speak. Watch yourself as you speak. Do you speak more than 50% of the time?

EFFECTIVE LISTENING

Speak Less
Respond, Not React
Respect Viewpoints

Respond: Do you react to people's comments even before they are finished? Let the person you are listening to finish what they have to say. Take a long, slow, and deep breath before you respond. If you notice yourself becoming very emotional while you're speaking, defer your response or at least dial back the energy in what you say. If you emotionally react in a way that makes people feel they are being attacked, they will stop sharing.

Respect: Cultivate different points of view in your business. Respect the diversity of the points of view on the challenges you face. Debates by talented people who can respectfully listen and respond to each other will lead to great solutions. Foster an environment that encourages people to provide alternate points of view.

CELEBRATE THE WINS

For decades I never experienced a sunrise. Then, I started doing overnight passages on sailboats. During the night, finding landmarks, tracking other boats, especially freighter traffic, and managing sails in the dark are huge challenges. When day breaks all of your problems seem to disappear. Huge freighters that seemed to loom on the radar suddenly look far away in the light of day. Keeping sail trim becomes a joy. On passage, the start of a new day is a big win.

We all have experiences where we suddenly realize that we have a sense of gratitude for what we have achieved. In a business context, we tend to get so wrapped up in our day-to-day fire fighting that we never pause to acknowledge our gratitude for what is working. Just like being on passage on a sailboat at night feels like one challenge after another, we need to find the equivalent of sunrise and daylight to have a sense of gratitude for what we have overcome.

To set the tone, be energized, and to feel a sense of gratitude I focus on the wins. Whether it is finishing tasks, teams that are working together, or time with the family focus your wins on:

- What is working?
- What did you achieve?
- What challenges did you overcome?

I start every week by writing down a list of my personal and professional wins. With a few minutes of reflection I am always amazed at how much is going right in my life. Where moments before I was mired in the week's challenges, after having acknowledged my wins, I am energized and in a completely different frame of mind to write down my weekly to-do list.

When working with teams, I insist that weekly planning meetings start with the wins. I get everyone to email their list of wins before the meeting. At the start of the meeting, I get each individual to provide 1-2 of their

> Positive psychology works. Start every day and every meeting with wins.

top wins from the previous week. The immediate challenges become much more manageable once you start from a position of success.

Because I do my best work when collaborating with others, sharing my list of wins also means that I get to express gratitude to those who helped me achieve those wins. Focusing on the positive and giving thanks always sets me up to tackle the inevitable challenges which lie ahead.

Sharing successes is an act of positive psychology. If you would like to learn more about the power of positive psychology, I recommend you check out Shawn Achor's book *The Happiness Advantage: The Seven Principles Of Positive Psychology That Fuel Success And Performance At Work.*

RHYTHM

I like to ski. Once you learn the technical aspects of skiing, great ski days become all about rhythm and flow, feeling the fall line of the mountain you are on, the conditions that day, and how your skis react to the snow. If you are carving turns with someone else, you need to get into his or her rhythm, too. The result can be the most amazing dance down the mountain.

Creating outstanding business performance requires you to build the rhythm and flow of the business and the individuals in the business, including you. One of the best ways to do that is through weekly team meetings. Pick the same day and time for the weekly meetings. Some like to use Friday afternoon to plan the next week. I personally like to get the initial fires out of the way on Monday mornings so my weekly team meetings can take place on Monday afternoon after lunch. These move to Tuesday if Monday is a holiday. Find what works for you and your team.

We've all been in boring meetings, so what kind of format makes weekly meetings more lively? After taking five minutes to share the wins, take five minutes to review your progress on your measurable quarterly goals. This reminds everyone to pull in the same direction and course correct through the quarter if things get off track. Keeping your quarterly goals firmly in mind, review what needs to get done for the week. Concentrate on the 3W's — Who, What, When.

3W'S

Who
What
When

Let everyone have his or her say, while being mindful of the time. Encourage debate—that is why you have the best talent in the room together for a weekly meeting. It is okay to disagree and even to disagree a lot. In the end, a plan needs to come together for the week.

In the last five minutes, wrap up and confirm all the Who, What, and Whens for the upcoming week. Make sure that every person states their #1 take away from the meeting so you are certain everyone is aligned on their work for the week.

CONSTANT COMMUNICATION

To employees, senior management appear as if they are on top of a mountain: isolated, separated from the rest of the company and making occasional pronouncements from on high. This applies even more to the CEO. While you might think you are being clear, your messages can often sound like the teacher in Charlie Brown's classroom—"wha, wha, wha."

Keep everyone moving together through clear and constant communication. These are techniques I've used to help with employee communication.

Management Focus: Great internal communication starts with clarity among the management team on what it is you are trying to achieve. If there is a lack of clarity at the top, it shows up in missing or muddy communications to everyone else.

Communicate Often: Numerous small communications are much better than sending out an "employee newsletter" once a quarter. Constant communication lets employees see that you care. It also ties communications to recent events, helping to keep your most important priorities as top of mind awareness among your employees.

Where's the boss: The activities of the CEO provide the strongest guidance to employees as to what is important to the company. If you are CEO, share a weekly list of key activities you are planning, especially if those include travel, industry events, and customer visits. A daily or weekly "Where's the CEO posting" can be an effective way to let people know what you are focusing your energy on.

A single voice: To provide clarity, a single person should be responsible for communicating to all your employees. This keeps the tone and content consistent, while ensuring that the right messages are flowing from you to all the individuals in the organization.

THINK AND TALK BIG

You are what you believe. If the people in an organization think the company is small, they will act that way. If they think the company is big, they will act that way. It all comes down to belief.

I remember once working with a CEO who called the company "little" while giving his monthly speech to all his employees. At the same company, I heard the VP of Sales tell his sales team during a quarterly planning session that the company is "small".

The company had more than a decade-long track record, with thousands of customers, incredible products and fabulous customer stories. Yet, the senior leaders were still referring to the company as "small".

In the twenty years I spent at Robelle, we never thought of ourselves as small. We would show up at trade shows with our 10 X 20 booth, while the "big ones" spent hundreds of thousands of dollars on enormous booths and displays. While our booth would be lined up with customers and prospects theirs would be empty. Our booth was filled with talented individuals who answered any technical and business questions thrown our way. People came away from the "big ones" wondering if anyone in the company had any product or solution knowledge. It all came down to what we believed, as what we believed determined how we acted. How we acted was how we were perceived. Talk like you are big and you will be big.

KEEPING YOUR EDGE

The steepest run on Blackcomb Mountain in Whistler, BC is called the Blow Hole. Located at the top of Blackcomb Glacier, you have to take four lifts and hike the last ten minutes to get to it.

Standing on the lip of the Blow Hole always makes a small pit form in my stomach, no matter how well I am skiing. One year, my first time down the Blow Hole that season, I fell on the second turn, losing one of my skis. With a 54-degree slope, I was at the very bottom before I could stop myself. Thankfully, a better skier stopped at the top, collected my ski, and brought it down to me. Having been humbled by the mountain, I put my ski back on and skied the five miles (eight kilometers) down the rest of the run.

Why challenge myself by skiing down the steepest run on Blackcomb Mountain? To keep my edge honed. By challenging myself in one area of my life, I improve the capabilities I bring to the other areas of my life. If I ace the run, the sense of accomplishment I feel gives me confidence to reach new limits in my professional and personal life.

To reach our maximum potential, entrepreneurs need to constantly be looking for our edge. And if sometimes you fall down, it teaches you that you can fail, get up, dust yourself off, and try again.

TAKING THINGS FOR GRANTED

Early on the morning of May 14, 2013 I ran with a friend next to the ocean on Spanish Banks, a beach near our home in Vancouver, BC. As I got in the car after the run, I was a little dizzy. I drove through a parking lot next to the beach, which started to feel like it was undulating underneath me. I drove another block before my whole world felt like giant ocean waves were moving the car and me in dizzying circles. It was all I could do to safely pull to the curb and stop.

After both doctor and hospital visits, I was diagnosed with vertigo induced by an inner ear viral infection. While I have sailed over 15,000 nautical miles and experienced seasickness numerous times, suffering vertigo in a perfectly still car scared me and caused me to experience true vulnerability. Even three weeks later, I was only able to do a short run and walk on the beach.

This experience taught me that there is much that I take for granted. It also taught me that I have an incredible support network. Other things I learned from this experience:

> **Power:** I am blessed with powerful energy, coordination, and physical strength. Most often, I take these for granted. This experience taught me that these are amazing gifts that I have been given and which can be taken away at a moment's notice.

> **Support:** I have the loving support of Karalee and my three children, Jocelyn, Kevin, and Allen. All shared their strength and presence with me as I recovered from this experience. We are also fortunate to live in British Columbia, which has a publicly funded healthcare system. When I needed the system, it was there, in spades, to look after me.

> **Vulnerabilities:** We are human and as human beings we all have our vulnerabilities. When we are vulnerable, we rely on others. As

a driven individual who often tries to "do it all myself", it was good for me to have to ask for and rely on other people. We all need to rely on other people, whether we admit it or not.

Healing: As an individual who often lives for the next action, I learned to stay out of action in order to heal. Work had to be put on hold, and I needed to stay still and rest. My need to take on the next goal had to be tempered with listening to my body and staying in the moment.

You will have personal experiences that test your endurance or family events that will keep you out of your business for a time. Know that if you ask for help, the help will be there. Take the time needed to look after yourself and your loved ones.

AN IDEAL DAY

As entrepreneurs, we start our own businesses so that we can have the life we want. Then, we get so caught up in our business that we forget what an ideal day looks like. Family, travel, my wife, Karalee, our three children, Jocelyn, Kevin, and Allen, connection, food,

What does your ideal day look like?

time, photography, music, and gratitude are all part of my ideal day. I am fortunate that some parts of my ideal day are part of my regular day.

Define your ideal day. Write it down. Make sure that some aspects of your ideal day show up every day for you in business and in life.

SHINY RED BALL DISTRACTIONS

As entrepreneurs, we are hardwired to focus on what is new and exciting. If we see a shiny red ball, we will be distracted. Shiny red balls distract many high performing people, myself included. While playing with a ball can be invigorating, more often than not it proves to be a distraction. What can you do if you feel yourself being lured by the next shiny red ball?

Strategy: Red balls are opportunities that pass by us. When feeling the distraction, return to the strategic focus you have set for yourself. This reminds you why you are doing what you do, grounding you back to your strategic plan.

Challenge: If you are feeling overwhelmed or challenged, a bright new idea may seem like an easier path than the one you are on. Reach into your toolkit and do those things that renew your energy. I ski, sail, photograph, spend time with my family, or just spend time in nature. Find out what works for you.

Momentum: As humans we always overestimate what we can do in three months and underestimate what we can do in two years. The key is to stay true to your vision. If you keep going step-by-step, you will be amazed at how far you can go by maintaining your focus.

Leadership: Where you go the rest of your team follows. If you are constantly changing direction to chase the next opportunity, your team will be left uncertain and confused. Keeping your focus allows them to keep their focus. Even if you are uncertain, continuing to move towards your vision inspires confidence in everyone around you.

CHALLENGES ARE OPPORTUNITIES

What I have learned is that every challenge is an opportunity. As an entrepreneur, the next challenge may be something I need to learn from. In an organization, a challenging situation often shows which individuals will bubble to the top. Challenges can be an incredible proving ground for talented individuals to grow into the next level of their career, bringing the company with them.

It can be hard. I know from past experience that this will pass over time. When everything seems foggy and out of focus in the moment, it eventually comes into focus and the fog does lift. Pushing through it all is the challenge.

As entrepreneurs some of the biggest mistakes we make with challenges include:

- Trying to solve it all on our own. This is a time to work with your senior management team, advisors, and especially your employees to find solutions.

- Even in the most difficult challenges, pause for a moment. Not only will your response be better, it is more likely that you might see the edges of what could be an opportunity.

MENTORS AND CEO PEER GROUPS

While being an entrepreneur can feel lonely you don't have to be alone. There are many peer networking groups for entrepreneurs. Find one that appeals to you, then make the commitment to become part of the group. This typically means showing up for monthly meetings, and sharing openly and honestly about your challenges, while listening and responding to the others in the group. I've found that it takes about a year for an entrepreneur peer group to completely gel and trust one another. Building that trust is key to creating a safe environment for you to share problems and receive advice. Find your peer group and put in the time and effort to make it successful—for you and the others in your group.

> Surround yourself with peers who can support you through thick and thin.

Case Study:
BOB PARK, PRESIDENT & CEO, FINCAD

"All businesses are people businesses."
– Bob Park, President & CEO, Fincad

Bob Park is an entrepreneur who has overcome numerous challenges and changes in the twenty-five years since he co-founded Fincad. Bob and his original partner started the business in 1990 in the early stages of the modern over-the-counter financial derivatives business. Coming from the brokerage industry, they saw that there was a tremendous imbalance between what the derivatives experts in the big banks knew and what their clients, mainly non-financial companies, knew. As a result, the corporate treasurers and CFOs of those customer organizations were making costly mistakes or even being cheated. Bob and his partner set out to level the playing field by providing the customers of the banks with the knowledge and technology needed to deal in the derivatives markets in an informed way. Bob started with almost no money and has weathered stormy periods to reinvent himself and his company.

BACKGROUND

Fincad created and sold Fincad Analytics Suite, a Microsoft Excel plug-in that can be applied to a wide variety of markets and problems. Their solution applied specialized financial mathematics to value or assess the risk from changes in interest rates, foreign exchange rates, volatility, and credit defaults. Bob quickly realized that in order to be successful, they would need to focus on the corporate participants in the derivatives markets, almost all of whom were thousands of miles from Fincad's office.

Unable to raise any venture capital money, Bob boot strapped Fincad. He sold his house and used his retirement savings, line of credit and credit cards to start selling initial versions of the software. Lacking the money to open remote sales offices they began with an inside telephone sales model, an unheard of way to sell business to business software at the time. They also pioneered the concept of try before you buy and were one of the first to have a store front on the Internet. As Fincad grew, over 90% of their business came from outside Canada.

A NEW CHALLENGE

While Bob and his partner had overcome numerous challenges in starting and growing Fincad, by the mid-2000s Bob had begun to feel something was wrong. He had an intuitive sense that his sales team wasn't performing to their potential. Fincad made the decision to invest in a top-to-bottom review of their sales, hiring the sales experts of The Alexander Group to analyze and report on all aspects of their selling.

The report was critical of the entire organization including Bob and the senior management team. From strategy to the nuts and bolts of their sales operations, there were problems everywhere. They had no global sales strategy. Their inside telephone sales team was spending less than an hour and a half on the phone a week. Not a day, a week. They were trying to do all their business via email. When measured, it was found that they spent 37% of their time doing service work like moving software licenses from machine to machine.

The report identified their lack of engagement with their prospects on their business problems as the root cause of their sales challenges. Most of their leads were coming from natural search on the Internet. Prospects were looking for a point solution to manage their risk and Fincad had just the product they needed. Their inside sales team serviced these sales, generating continuous revenue growth, yet Bob and the Fincad team had little knowledge of the actual business problems they were solving for their customers. The core problem was that Fincad was feature-focused and not solution-focused in everything they did, from marketing to selling.

MELTDOWN AND CHANGE

Just as Bob and his team were grappling with everything the sales review report had revealed, the 2008 financial crisis hit them. There was a six-month period in late 2008 and early 2009 where no one in Fincad's markets was buying anything. Bob had to make the difficult decision to lay some people off.

In analyzing their revenue, Bob and his team realized that many customers were not renewing their support. Their business model was based on Microsoft's model. They sold perpetual software licenses to organizations on a per user basis and charged for the first year's support, all for an upfront fee. They released new versions of Fincad Analytics Suite every year and then charged users a discounted price to upgrade to the new version. Because they built such reliable software, less than 20% would renew support after the compulsory first year and only 25% would purchase software upgrades in any given year. Even Fortune 500 customers would sometimes go six or eight years without purchasing an upgrade.

Bob saw an opportunity to change this model. During the downturn they modified their business model to be subscription-based. Users would still be purchasing licenses, but these would only be valid for one to three years. To entice existing users to the new model, they offered 70% discounts on a time-limited basis. The inside sales team were kept busy finding customers and interacting with them, converting them to the new license model throughout the three-year transition. These changes saw Fincad through the 2010 to 2012 period, keeping cash flow steady with the sales of the new license model. Post-crisis new sales were still few and far between, with revenue dropping by about 45% in the middle of the process and losses mounting.

The learning curve was steep. The financial crisis led to massive change in the financial industry. The inside sales team hadn't kept up and were out of touch with their accounts. In one case an account manager called an Asian bank customer to get a license renewal only to learn that the entire team had moved to a different bank more than a year before. This was a direct result of only calling customers a few months before the end of a license term.

Because inside sales now phone all current and former customers on a continuous basis, they are starting to learn a lot more about what their customers do and how they use Fincad's software. Fincad's clients were previously under-served. Now, through proper account management, they are finding out which accounts are at risk in advance instead of when it is too late.

A NEW STRATEGY

After about fifteen years in business, Bob made the critical decision to take everything they had learned and move in a new direction. Rather than continue to focus on a point solution with limited stickiness with customers, Fincad embarked on and invested in an ambitious project to develop an entirely new, legacy-free enterprise product called F3. F3 is an innovative and sophisticated product line with a price point and value proposition that is more than five times greater than Fincad Analytics Suite. F3 is targeted at enterprises that need to manage risk with multi-asset class portfolios.

In 2005 the derivatives markets were booming. There were many new complex instruments invented that were loosely called 'structured products'. An example of a structured product would be a bond that returned the minimum of either a guaranteed interest rate or the return of a stock index. Fincad were having trouble keeping their analytics up with the pace of financial innovation. Every investment bank put a new wrinkle in their new structured products. To support each of these new products, Fincad would need to sit down and start from scratch to write a new algorithm.

Bob and his team realized that they needed a better, faster, more efficient development method. Serendipitously, Bob ran into a senior developer with quantitative financial expertise at a major bank in London. He wanted to immigrate to Canada, which he could do two or three years sooner if he worked for Fincad. Bob set him up in a little skunk works and together with others on the team they invented F3.

NEW SALES TEAM

Developing F3 has required Bob and the Fincad team to gain a deep understanding of the actual business problems that their customers are trying to solve. Bob has started to build a global field sales team with in-depth domain knowledge. These sales professionals are backed up by experienced sales engineers who understand both the F3 technology and how F3 is effectively applied to specific risk-analysis problems.

Bob's sales management team has reorganized how they think and operate their entire sales. Inside sales teams consist of both a renewal team and a new sales team. The renewal team does not do expansion but refers those opportunities to the new sales team. The new sales team sells to new names and does expansion sales with existing customers.

While building a field sales team with extensive financial knowledge and contacts in their territories, Fincad has also transitioned their top performing inside sales team who are able to comprehend customers' financial challenges. These individuals are able to position and sell F3 as a complete solution in areas where they have not yet built a field sales force.

MORE CHANGE

Bob realized that in the past he didn't hire people with the experience needed for the job. He sees this as a typical small business challenge for entrepreneurs—you put somebody in place and you expect them to learn on the job because experienced people are more expensive. In addition to their new marketing, sales, and product strategy, they are going with a completely different approach to hiring. Fincad is hiring seasoned sales professionals in London and New York with the experience and contacts needed to sell F3 successfully. Bob has also made further changes to the management team, hiring senior leaders with proven experience and track records.

LESSONS LEARNED

For Bob, it has been an amazing ride. After almost twenty-five years in business, he continues to change both himself and his business. Bob is in the middle of these changes and is hopeful that they will produce amazing results. No matter how it turns out, I learned this from him:

1. It takes perseverance to last over the long term. Even when Bob and his team were uncertain about what to do next, they went forward and tried something new, pushing through their uncertainties.

2. Markets change—you have to be prepared to change with them.

3. Bob has the humility to admit that he doesn't know it all. He brought in outside expertise and took it on the chin when the analysis included mistakes in his own decisions.

4. The growth of Fincad highlights how Bob realizes that what got them to where they are today is not what will take them to the next level. He is fearless about bringing in others to elevate his and the company's strategy and performance.

As entrepreneurs we all have much to learn from Bob's experience. Growing a business requires that we look at ourselves and change the way we make decisions.

TAKE ACTION NOW

How you manage yourself and your life has a huge impact on your business. Building daily, weekly, and quarterly rhythms keeps you at peak performance. Being clear on what an ideal day is for you will help you clear away the clutter that is dragging you down. If everyone is pulling in the same direction, you dramatically improve the chance of making progress. Use these three actions to create momentum for you, your team, and your business:

1. Create a daily, weekly, monthly and quarterly rhythm for yourself. Write it down and stick with it.

2. Define your ideal day and then ensure that you live an aspect of your ideal day every day.

3. Within the next week, ask your first reports what they think the strategy for the quarter is. Use their feedback to improve your communication to them and the rest of your organization.

CORPORATE STRATEGY

When you set off on a sailboat adventure, you can jump onboard, cast off the lines, and take off. I remember once doing this with Karalee when we were sailing from Victoria to the southern Gulf Islands in British Columbia on our small Catalina 27 sailboat Fire Dragon. It was a bright sunny day; we had a chart and knew where we were going. We assumed that the weather in Victoria would be the same weather we would encounter on the rest of the journey.

If we had listened to the weather report, something every mariner knows to do, we would have heard that a huge wind was building. We were hit with this wind in the middle of our passage. Fire Dragon was completely overwhelmed—we ended up doing an accidental 360-degree turn before we even got the sails released. Then, we started the arduous process of getting the big genoa sail down and the small blade up as the waves built, throwing us around the boat as Fire Dragon heaved up and down in the waves, making me seasick. We could have easily handled the wind if we had planned for it from the beginning by thinking strategically about all the parts of our journey and listening to the weather forecast.

THREE-YEAR VISION

In running a business, it is often easy to be like Karalee and me when we set off on Fire Dragon. See a need, create a product, and cast off. What more planning do you need?

In 1979, I joined a young software startup as the first hire after the founders Robert and Annabelle. The company was named Robelle for the founders and was an incredible success story in the HP 3000 minicomputer market.

For many years, we built a business plan that was based on improving what we had done the previous year. Then, I brought in some outside strategic experts who suggested that I start thinking about the future of the business by planning out at least three years and then working backward to the current year and then to the current quarter. This approach fundamentally changed the way I looked at business strategy. Looking out three years in advance is the equivalent to considering what the weather might be like on your passage.

> Start with a **3-YEAR VISION** of where you are going.

PURPOSE

Jim Collins, author of *Good to Great*, would call it purpose. Guy Kawasaki in *The Art of the Start* asks us to act with meaning by creating a product or service that makes the world a better place.

While you need to be clear where you will be in three years, what markets you will be serving, and what your brand promise is (more on that later), people are motivated by having meaning in their lives. Since many people spend much of their lives at work, you will only get high performance when you, your management team, and your employees are aligned in the purpose and culture of your organization.

As Jim Collins states in the article "Aligning Action and Values"[1], it is not sufficient to document your purpose and core values. You must have specific measures and actions that demonstrate that people are living and in alignment with your purpose.

---

1   www.jimcollins.com/article_topics/articles/aligning-action.html

CULTURE

Intentionally or otherwise, every organization has a culture. Top performing people work for organizations where the purpose, values, and culture of the organization match their personal belief system. Many entrepreneurs and leaders try to invent or impose cultural values on an organization. This is a mistake—the process involves discovering your cultural values and then building on them towards your purpose, creating plans that are in alignment with both.

To lead individuals and companies to top performance, culture has to be actively defined, communicated, and developed. This is not something you want to leave to chance.

For example, wanting, seeking, and acting on customer feedback is not natural for many people. It takes courage, persistence, and ownership of things that inevitably will go wrong. If you seek out customer feedback, good and bad, acknowledging your mistakes when things do not go right, customers will forgive you for just about anything. Building a culture that craves this sort of feedback and response starts with great leadership.

Lead your company culture by:

1. Documenting your key culture and values.
2. Seeking feedback on your own performance from employees, customers, and partners about how you represent your culture.
3. Hiring for culture first and skills second.
4. Get out of your office daily, walk among your employees, listen to them, and encourage them, making sure that your culture is apparent in your actions.

If you want proven processes, templates, and actions to put culture at the center of your organization I recommend that you read and implement the ideas from Chris Edmonds and his book *The Culture Engine*. Chris demonstrates how our behaviors define the culture of our organization. If we want different results, we need to change behaviors. If we want to change behaviors, we need to change the culture.

BRAND PROMISE

> High performing companies have a measurable **BRAND PROMISE** that they deliver on every single day.

Higher performing companies make bold promises and then back them up with the people and systems to deliver on those promises. At Provident Security, they guarantee they will be at your door in five minutes after your alarm goes off. Provident Security then back that up with a promise delivery system that actually monitors and ensures they are in fact always responding to their customer's door within five minutes of the alarm going off.

Entrepreneurs often start their business with a vision of how to change an industry. They need to back up their vision by coming up with, writing down, and committing to a measurable brand promise that will be true to their vision. Align all of your key stakeholders by creating an impactful brand promise and then holding yourself and your company accountable to it.

GROWTH

The process of figuring out where you want to go takes time and effort. Here is a way to think about planning that will help. High growth companies operate at five or ten times the speed of a regular company. If you want high performance results, you need to think and act like a high performance and high growth company. In these companies, one quarter is the same as one year in a regular company, so planning that you would need to do in a regular business, say once a year, needs to be done quarterly.

YEARLY, QUARTERLY, MONTHLY, AND WEEKLY PLANNING

As entrepreneurs, we inevitably get caught up in the running of our business. Deciding on strategy requires us to get out of the business to work on the business. You need to make the decision that this is going to happen. Schedule all of your strategy and planning meetings far in advance, mark them on your calendar, and do not book other things into those time slots.

Typical meeting times for strategic planning would be:

PLANNING
Yearly
Quarterly
Monthly
Weekly

- First time: Plan at least two full days.

- Yearly: At least one full day.

- Quarterly: Two-thirds to one full day.

- Monthly: Two to three hours to review strategy and course adjust. Typically you extend the weekly operational meeting and only spend the first 15-30 minutes on your usual operational review.

- Weekly: One to two hours focused on operational reviews of what is on track and then debate, discuss, and make decisions on what to adjust for the next week to stay on track with your quarterly and yearly goals.

Planning meetings needs to be scheduled around the natural rhythms of your business. Every business has busier and slower times. Planning must be done so that you have enough time in advance to integrate what you choose into your business operations, though not so far in advance that you do not have enough feedback from your current operations. As the entrepreneur, you have to own the final accountability for finding those dates, getting them in everyone's calendar, and holding everyone responsible for showing up.

EVERYTHING IS AN EXPERIMENT

Kevin Lawrence, entrepreneur and coach[2], often reminds me that in business, as in life, everything is an experiment. If we go into our planning sessions with this attitude, we focus less on individual achievements (or lack thereof) and more on what experiments are working and what are not. The key is that we have our goals for the quarter to refer back to. And the measures we use throughout the quarter to measure our progress against our goals.

....
2   www.coachkevin.com

SET GOALS

In fifteen or twenty years, why will someone care about your business? This is a strategic question that should paint the big picture for why you, your team, your employees, and your stakeholders will stay in the game for the long term.

BHAG: What is your Big Hairy Audacious Goal (BHAG)? What actions will show that you are living your values and reaching for your BHAG? Jim Collins reminds us in *Built to Last: Successful Habits of Visionary Companies* that a BHAG needs to compel everyone to move towards a clear focal point. Your BHAG needs a measurable goal so that everyone will know when they have crossed the finish line.

Measurable Outcomes: Where do you want to be in 3-5 years? What markets are you in? How do you define those markets? What is your measurable brand promise?

One Year Goals: What are the five key one-year revenue, profit, margin, and other key measures? What are the five key initiatives that you will achieve in the next year? What are one or two key productivity indicators you will measure?

Quarterly Plan: What are the three goals that must be achieved for the next quarter? Who will be the single person held accountable for each of the goals? What are the key measures that will be tracked to ensure the whole company is on track to achieve the quarterly and yearly goals?

If you take the time and effort to answer these questions, write them down, and then keep everyone aligned to those goals, you will see magic happen. As I've seen over and over it can make the difference between poor or average performance and outstanding performance.

ALIGNMENT

I sometimes volunteer to drive race officials at Dragonboat regattas. This gives me the opportunity to sit back and observe the start of a

Dragonboat race. At the start of a Dragonboat race the starter brings all the Dragonboats up to the start line. Once the starter gets every boat in position in perfect order on the start line, they call out:

"We have alignment."

In working with business leaders I often wish that I could call out "We have alignment". In order to have alignment, you have to start with your limited set of yearly and quarterly goals. Then, you must keep yourself, your senior management team, and your employees accountable to these goals.

> **Accountability:** Clear lines of accountability must be a set. Groups, entities, and concepts cannot be held accountable. Only a person can be held accountable. For every critical project and responsibility there must be one person who accounts for their performance to the rest of the team. This person will rarely have direct control over all the people reaching for the goal. They do have the responsibility to know what is going on and report when things are not on track.

> **Rewards:** Have you ever seen a senior management team set goals for the year without changing their bonus and reward structure, tying it directly to the goals? Accountability and leadership have to start at the top. You need to create rewards throughout the organization so that everyone is being rewarded fairly for the goals that are being set.

MOMENTUM

In Jim Collins's book *Good to Great* he spends an entire chapter building a metaphor of business as a huge flywheel. Thousands and thousands of pounds of flywheel (kilograms for the rest of the world) that is hardly moving, if at all. Now start pushing on the flywheel. For a long time little or nothing happens.

If you push long enough eventually you will make a breakthrough. Momentum starts helping you instead of hindering you. Collins reminds us that we will never know which push was the final one that got the flywheel moving. It doesn't matter, because it was getting everyone to push together in the same direction that created the momentum.

Set no more than five goals. Get everyone aligned to those goals with accountability and rewards. This will get everyone to push in the same direction. Sooner or later the flywheel will break free and create momentum.

GET OUT OF THE OFFICE

If there is one thing you take away from this chapter, let it be that you must get out of the office to work on plans. Remember that the process is to look three years ahead, decide where you want to be, then work backwards to what you have to do this year, and then decide on what to do this quarter. At quarterly planning sessions, you need to evaluate what is working and what is not from the last quarter, using that information to plan where you need to go in the next quarter based on your goals for the year and for three years from now.

For years, I had all of the brainstorming and notes from strategic planning sessions typed up and organized. What I discovered is that I never used those notes nor did anyone else. The goal is to have everything documented in two to three pages: your company purpose, key cultural traits, your brand promise, three-year goals, one-year goals, and quarterly goals.

LOOK FOR OUTSIDE HELP

All of us get centered on our own issues and become myopic. For your strategic retreats, hire a facilitator who can bring an independent perspective to your business. A good facilitator will help extract information from each participant. They will drive everyone to come up with a very short (never more than five) list of measurable targets that must be accomplished in a quarter.

BUSINESS MODEL

Does everyone in your business understand your business model? Can you explain it in 30 seconds? Do you know where new business comes from versus business from existing customers?

It takes ten times more effort to land a new customer than it does to sell to an existing one. Does your business model include recurring revenue or many upselling opportunities? Sales is hard work. No matter what the size of the sales, the sales effort involved stays roughly the same.

Even if you start your business with a product that needs to be sold over and over, look for opportunities to sell to your existing customers. Ideas include:

> **BUSINESS MODEL**
> Explain yours to anyone in 30 seconds

- Rent instead of sell. You can now rent Apple computers, getting an upgrade every two years, for the same cost as purchasing a new one. For the retailers, this provides a more predictable revenue stream. It also gets you in the store every two years, where there are then opportunities to upsell you accessories.

- Look at other industries. How do they package and sell their products and services? What could you learn from them about new approaches to your business model?

- Split your product into reusable and consumable pieces. Razor blades are a classic example of this strategy.

The core of your market strategy must account for how and how often you must sell your products and services. This sales process must be included in your models for the cost of sales and repeat business. Your business model must account for how you sell, what form the revenue takes, how you collect the revenue, and how much it costs you to deliver your brand promise for the revenue you are generating.

Case Study:
BOB GRAHAM, FOUNDER AND CEO AIRWAVES MUSIC

Bob Graham is a classic entrepreneur who started his first enterprise mowing lawns and teaching guitar in his neighborhood. After a succession of jobs, Bob realized he only had one life to live. A chance encounter led him to found Airwaves Music and grow it into Canada's leading DJ company.

BACKGROUND

Bob has always worked hard at everything he has pursued. While successful at dozens of jobs, he was never fulfilled in any of them. He learned guitar as a teenager, played in bands, and was hired by a former boss to play at his daughter's wedding. Shortly afterwards Bob met up with Lester, a friend of his who worked as a DJ. While Bob made around $150 as a classical guitarist playing at weddings, he learned that Lester made $1,000 per wedding. Lester's problem was that he wasn't familiar with the business of running a company or marketing his DJ services.

Sensing an opportunity, Bob made a deal with Lester. He would market Lester's DJ services and they would split the fees. Bob realized his purpose was to help his friend, while also helping customers who needed DJ services. While Bob started opportunistically without a plan, his focus on outstanding customer experience made Lester and him successful. This success led to Bob founding and growing Airwaves Music.

PROFESSIONALISM

Bob is methodical. He initially made a list of all the things he would change about the DJ experience couples had at their wedding. If the wedding was at a 5-star hotel, he wanted Lester to be dressed just like the staff members who would be looking after the wedding in the hotel. He surveyed clients after their wedding to see what they thought of their DJ experience and continues to seek feedback from all of his customers today.

After a couple of years, Bob was growing the business fast enough so that Lester couldn't fulfill all their commitments on his own. From 8-9 gigs in his first year, they did 31 gigs in their second. Bob then made a breakthrough discovery—none of the high quality, local DJ companies ever worked with multiple DJs. Bob then made it his mission to prove that it was possible to run an exceptional company with multiple DJs on the roster in multiple cities. He then started a process to discover and work with the very best DJs in Vancouver.

WORLD CLASS DJS

Bob's brand promise is "Your Music, Your Way". He relentlessly focuses Airwaves Music on being the most trusted, reliable, and respected DJ service in the country. Bob's long-term goal is to deliver these promises as the largest DJ music company in all of Canada. Bob believes that his customers have to feel a personal affinity for the DJ they hire to have an outstanding experience. His hiring, evaluation, and ongoing review of both his DJs and customer surveys keep Bob focused on delivering a minimum 9 out of 10 experience, always striving for perfection—10/10 customer experiences.

In addition to delivering world-class DJ experiences to people getting married, Bob has had to build first-rate systems. Margins are thin in the DJ business. Bob found an outstanding mentor through the Entrepreneur's Organization who could work with Bob to build a financial model that would give Bob insight into the key factors in his business, while ensuring that he continues to be profitable.

SUPPORT NETWORK

A key moment in Bob's journey with Airwaves Music was being introduced to the founder and CEO of one of the largest construction companies in North America. Bob got 30 minutes with the CEO, who told him to keep a little black notebook with three intertwined lists, written out in as much detail as possible:

1. Bob's to-do list,
2. His dreams, and
3. His measurable goals.

Bob used this idea to think of what he wanted and then to write down in detail exactly what he wanted his and Airwaves Music's future to look like. Bob stays in touch with the construction CEO, who continues to advise him and who has become a trusted friend. He also joined the Entrepreneur Organization, meeting once a month with his peers to get feedback and to learn from the group's shared experiences. Drawing from this network has helped Bob avoid numerous pitfalls and mistakes in his business and ultimately has changed his life.

THE RIGHT PEOPLE

Bob spends a lot of time finding and hiring the right people. Everyone in the industry told Bob that not only was it impossible to have a DJ company with multiple DJs, he could never use a site like Craigslist to advertise and attract DJs. While Bob does attract DJs through word-of-mouth, he also uses Craigslist to advertise for DJs. Bob used Brad Smart's Topgrading techniques to develop and fine-tune his interview and audition process.

In every city in which Airwaves Music operates, Bob holds events to bring the over 300 DJs in the Airwaves family together. They are a unique tribe who relate to each other. He has harnessed the power of social media, creating a Facebook group exclusively for Airwaves Music DJs across Canada. One of Bob's key measures is how many of his DJs are liking and commenting on their DJ Facebook group.

Bob has brought equal discipline to hiring sales people. In a low margin business where he sells an intangible product, he pays his sales people on a 100% commission basis. He sells exclusively through telesales with his sales people in Vancouver selling Airwaves Music services all across Canada. Bob attracts and motivates his sales staff by creating an opportunity for them to live a dream lifestyle where each sales person is in control of their destiny, being able to work hard for a period and then take a break to pursue their own dreams. Bob has built flexibility into his systems to make this a reality for the sales people who work with him.

MARKETING

Bob and his team used to attend hundreds of meetings at hotels and wedding fairs. These were expensive—he estimates that in one year he spent $40,000 on these events with a 10% ROI. His breakthrough was to give up all events and move to a purely online model.

He uses SEO, AdWords, and Facebook. Bob feels that Facebook is currently performing best. He says that AdWords can provide up to 400% ROI. His spending on online advertising is based on 10% of forecasted revenue.

Bob is investing heavily in high quality video and photos for his website. His focus is on young people, nationally. The majority of his customers are couples in their mid-twenties to early thirties who want a DJ for their wedding. Bob's videos convey the personalized experience that his DJs deliver each and every time for his customers' special day.

BY THE NUMBERS

Bob is ever curious about his business. He continuously experiments, measures, and revises his plans and systems. In addition to customer surveys and metrics from his DJ Facebook group, Bob tracks the number of DJs interviewed, hired, and how many complaints they receive. He keeps focused on his net profit margin by focusing on the list price, discount list, and margin quota for every sale. The reality is that some customers can easily afford his list price, while others will always try to push the price down.

For sales, Bob focuses on the number of leads, number of new leads, and revenue last year at this time versus revenue booked this year. He tracks their revenue growth and a key quality measure is the number of cancellations. Bob has discovered that the best times for calling are noon, 6 PM, and 2 PM on Saturdays. On average, each sale requires four touches with an average close time of two weeks. Even if a couple feels that a DJ delivered a 7 out of 10 experience at their wedding they may reduce or even not pay for their service if they are paying after the event. To eliminate this type of collections headache Bob made it a policy that all DJ services be 100% paid for two weeks prior to the event. After this, there were no more collection problems.

PERSONAL STRATEGY

Much of the growth of Airwaves Music has paralleled Bob's personal growth as a leader. He continues to use his personal notebook to track his to-do list, dreams, and goals. He is now aware of which "hat" he is wearing when he is operating the business, going as far as to create different email addresses for each "division". This helps remind Bob to act as the division head if he doesn't yet have a person in that role.

Once a week, Bob gets out of the office for four hours to focus on strategy. Once a quarter he steps back from the business to do his strategic planning, looking out over the next ten years. His goal is to continue to stay out of the business, focusing on these five aspects of his business:

1. Finding and keeping DJs.
2. Finding and keeping staff members.
3. Selling through advertising.
4. Selling through relationships.
5. Planning events.

FUTURE GROWTH

Bob continuously evolves his financial models and internal systems. His next big challenge is to choose and implement a better Customer Relationship Management (CRM) system for his business. His short-term goal is to grow to cover ten cities in Canada; then he plans to take his model to the US.

Couples need many services at their wedding. Bob is carefully building his systems so that in the future he can market and sell additional wedding services through the same platform and sales people. He is considering videographers and photographers as a potential target for his next phase of growth.

LESSONS LEARNED

Bob saw an opportunity, stepped into it, and created a fresh and inno- vative new way to meet the music needs of couples getting married in

Canada. From his early opportunistic success, Bob has grown the business strategically while staying true to his original purpose for founding Airwaves Music in the first place, providing us with these thoughts:

1. From the beginning, have a clear reason for what you are doing.

2. To accelerate growth, focus on the strategy, systems, and measures that drive your business.

3. Always stay curious, being prepared to continuously experiment, measure, and adjust your business as you grow.

4. Attract people who naturally fit together—both as customers of your service and as the providers of that service.

5. Stay focused on your long-term objectives, while being clear on what you need to measure today to be successful.

Bob has challenged an industry by putting together 300 outstanding DJs who deliver awesome wedding experiences to couples in Canada as well as nightclubs, restaurants, and top brands every day of the week.

TAKE ACTION NOW

Focusing on the reason you founded your business and where you want to be in ten, three, and one years will lead to long-term success. To make this happen you need to do consistent quarterly planning with measurable goals which will create a high growth, high performing business. Aligning yourself and your culture requires you to identify and write down your key values. Weekly meetings that encourage debate, while coming to agreement about what to be done next, keep everyone in alignment. This is challenging, so use these ideas to get you started.

1. Book a day within the next 60 days to take your entire senior management team off site to plan and document your ten, three, and one-year visions and goals.

2. Create and stick with a weekly management meeting that focuses on debate about where the business is going and agreement on how you will get there.

3. Write down the four or five key corporate values you hold. Every day find one example of how you and your management team are living your core values.

INNOVATION STRATEGY

I have been sailing since I was twelve. You might think that sailing has changed little over the last hundred years, but nothing could be further from the truth. Innovation has driven advances in materials, design, production, electronics and more. Navigation has changed almost beyond recognition.

Thirty years ago no one sailed across an ocean without a sextant. When I sailed across the Atlantic with my friend Dick Leighton recently, we had four GPS units on board, but not a single sextant. The way I use GPS has also evolved through innovation.

Today we take this for granted as we use mapping apps on our smartphones. In 2001, when we headed out for two years in the Mediterranean, charting software had advanced to the point that you could plot waypoints and routes on a digital map on a laptop. Our solution showed us our position and direction in real-time using a feed from one of our two onboard GPS units. We successfully navigated over 5,000 nautical miles (10,000 kilometers) in the Mediterranean with only a few references to paper charts. For emergencies, we did carry 1:300,000 charts of every place we went in the Med "just in case" our electronic solutions failed.

Today, almost all sailors navigate using electronic charts. Navigation in the entire boating industry has been changed in the span of only thirty years, driven by relentless innovation beginning with the invention of GPS systems.

COMPETITION

Whether innovation is a core part of your corporate strategy or not, you need to be proactive about the protection of your brand and intellectual property; if you don't, your competition likely will and this can put you in an untenable position.

Innovate or your competitors will get ahead

When Bob and Annabelle founded Robelle in 1977 their first product was Qedit. In the long history of the HP3000 minicomputer platform, Qedit was the leading integrated development environment for the market. Years and years of communication, marketing, and customer success cemented Qedit in the minds of HP3000 users.

By the mid-90s, we recognized the tremendous amount invested in the Qedit brand and took steps to register Qedit as a trademark in the US and Canada. In the meantime, another company had created a popular text editor for MS DOS also called Qedit. They were within one month of being granted the US trademark for Qedit.

We dodged the bullet of having our brand taken away because we were able to prove that we had been using the Qedit mark longer than the MS DOS Qedit. Bob Green met and negotiated with the owners of the MS DOS Qedit. He actually felt sorry for them—they were self-made entrepreneurs who had developed their Qedit much like Bob had developed his. But business is business and we had been the first to use the Qedit mark.

Our lesson in this is that if you don't protect your brands, copyright material, trade secrets, and intellectual property, there is a good chance that the competition can impede or even take away your brand equity if you haven't protected yourself. Use an innovation development and protection strategy to protect yourself and make it more difficult for your competitors to compete against you.

CHANGE AN INDUSTRY

Does your industry have a dirty little secret? Later in this book we showcase Mike Jagger and Provident Security. Mike's breakthrough was that in the alarm business customers had an expectation that when an alarm went off something would happen. The reality was that at best you got a phone call. Mike made the decision to turn his industry on its head and made the outrageous brand promise that they would be at their customer's door within five minutes of an alarm going off—guaranteed.

In the example of Bob Graham and Airwaves Music in the previous chapter, he was told that high quality DJ companies could never work with multiple DJs. Bob proved them wrong, building one of the most successful DJ companies in Canada. Discover the untold secret of your industry; innovate around that problem, leaving competitors in your dust.

LOOK OUTSIDE YOUR INDUSTRY

Innovative ideas are everywhere, except perhaps inside your company. We all end up with blinders. The trick is to find fresh new sources for ideas.

Look outside your industry for new methods, models, processes, and technology that can be applied to your business. If your products are based on a particular technology or process, seek out the best experts in the world on the framework you use. Get to know these people, read their writing, and leverage their expertise to provide you with new ways of looking at and solving problems.

CUSTOMERS

Customers often know more about your products than you do. Use them as a source of inspiration and ideas for product development. It's simple—just ask them. Your customers will be flattered and you will have a completely new source of ideas.

Create focus groups within your key market segments. Invite representative customers to become part of a focus group for that market. Meet with them quarterly by phone and once a year face-to-face. Customers in your focus group are particularly keen to gain access to more information about your products and plans. Use the face-to-face meetings to gain insight into where your customers see their business and markets moving in the short- and medium-term.

INDUSTRY PEERS

In the HP3000 marketplace where Robelle specialized, a group of us got together once a year for a two-day face-to-face meeting. This included many of our competitors, key thought leaders in the industry, and representatives from HP itself (makers of the HP3000). We started with no agenda, brainstormed ideas, agreed on the length of the topics, and then voted as a group on what we would talk about. This was a powerful way to discover the key issues in the marketplace year after year.

Our peer group meeting worked because together we took the view that we were all trying to grow the HP3000 market to make it bigger. You may avoid your competitors and other key leaders in your industry. My experience is that you have more to gain by being friends with them than viewing them as the enemy. Comparing notes appropriately with the key players in your industry is a powerful way to gain insight into markets and where you need to innovate.

PROTECTION

You must decide how to protect your intellectual property. In some cases, you may decide to keep some of your processes and technology as trade secrets. This works as long as no competitor is granted a patent that would force you to stop using your process or technology.

> You decide how much to protect your intellectual property

You will need to decide on your protection strategy based on trade secrets, patents, trademarks, and copyrights. Each has its own jurisdiction, process, and best practices. We will provide an overview here, but the key is to decide on how much time and effort your overall corporate and product strategy is based on innovation, protection, and branding. Use this overview to help get you started, but find and hire the right experts to protect your intellectual property.

JURISTICTION

Patent, trademark, and copyright laws are specific to every country in the world. Protect your intellectual property by thinking first about which countries you want to have room to practice in first. Use the industry, segmentation, and geographic characteristics from the Marketing chapter to work out where you need to begin with your intellectual property protection.

KEEPING YOUR RIGHTS

In most jurisdictions, there is the notion that patents, copyrights, trademarks, and other intellectual property is owned by the company when an employee has created the work. If there are no employment agreements in place, there are many grey areas where you may not end up owning the intellectual property you paid for. It is important that your employee agreements include specific clauses that assign all work the employee does on behalf of the company to the company. If you use subcontractors to create anything on your company's behalf, make sure that your agreements include specific clauses assigning all intellectual property rights to the company. It is often the case that subcontractors own the rights to what they create, unless there is an agreement in place that specifically states otherwise. This is one area where you must get legal advice to protect your company's rights and property.

PATENTS

A patent grants you the exclusive right for a limited amount of time (typically twenty years) to protect your invention. In exchange, you must publicly declare all aspects of your invention. Many people believe that patents are designed to prevent innovation. The exact opposite is true. By granting the patent holder exclusive time-limited rights, the details of the invention must be disclosed. This information then gives others a chance to invent a way around the patent, leveraging the knowledge shared in the patent.

When applying for a patent, you must cite all prior art in the field. Your new patent must be different from all preexisting patents covering the same type of invention. It is critical that if you rely on inventions for your products, you understand the patent landscape so you do not inadvertently use someone else's invention.

When introducing new innovations and products, you must file your patent application before any public use, commercialization or publication of the invention. It is important that all of your employees recognize and agree to confidentiality agreements. In today's connected world, it is easy for some aspects of the invention to be written about accidently in a public forum. Keep the information inside your company until you are ready to file your patents.

Costs for patents are dependent on how much of the work you and your team are prepared to do. If the people doing the inventing complete most of a patent application, legal advice is only needed to review the application, remove limiting language, and do the filing (including filing fees). For a single patent in one jurisdiction, this can range from $7,500-30,000US. If a legal team has to video the engineers working at a white board and then translate that into a patent application, the costs can easily be in the hundreds of thousands of dollars.

Best practices for innovative companies aim to motivate employees with cash compensation and recognition within the company on patent filing and when patents are awarded. Typically, one to two thousand dollars to each engineer who worked on the patent application when it is filed and the same amount again when the patent is granted.

TRADEMARKS

Trademarks are literally marks used in the trade of goods. At Robelle, one of our product lines was Qedit. When we sent a tape with the Qedit software on it, we put a label on the tape that said Qedit. When the customer received the tape it was the physical good that was used in trade. It was marked with Qedit, so Qedit was the mark used in trade. You back this up by

> Trademarks are literal. The marks you use when doing "trade".

using the same name in quotes, invoices, and in all communication with the client.

There are two types of trademarks: word and design. In the example above, Qedit is a word and that was the word trademark we applied for and were granted. We also had a cute visual logo for Qedit. This design mark must be trademarked separately from your word mark.

When coming up with product names and logos, spend time searching the trademark databases of the jurisdiction you plan to sell your products in. If you use someone else's trademark, you run the real risk of having them sue you. Trademarks apply to specific goods and services in specific markets. If your goods, services, or markets are substantially different from those marks already registered, you may be able to register your desired mark.

In our modern world an increasing number of our trademarks appear online only. There are provisions in most trademark acts to handle this. You should be certain to protect those marks that you are using online, including web pages, smartphone apps, and login screens. These are the goods your customers are purchasing and are thus used in trade and should be trademarked. Most domain name authorities grant additional rights to trademark holders in the jurisdictions in which they operate. Just because you have a domain name does not guarantee that you can keep it if someone else can demonstrate that they own the trademark.

Trademark agents can be a cost effective way to do trademark searches and to register trademarks. These are companies that specialize in the entire process. You do not have to use your legal firm to do your trademark protection. In many cases, a trademark agent will have more in-depth and broader experience than your lawyers. Either way, make sure that the experts you are working with have expertise in the jurisdictions you want to operate in.

COPYRIGHT

We often think of copyright protection in terms of music, movies, and books. Much of the material you produce may also be protected by copyright. Some examples include:

- Software
- Publications (white papers, reference material)
- Marketing materials
- Web site content

While copyright protection is automatic once a work is created, best practices should specifically include a copyright notice in all copyrighted work. While this does little to legally protect you, it signals to everyone working on the copyrighted material that your company owns the copyright to the material. The copyright notice is the word "Copyright" or the © symbol, followed by the first year of creating, and then the name of the legal entity which owns the copyright (typically your legal company name).

Additional rights are granted when you register your copyrighted work with a copyright office in a jurisdiction where you operate. If you make substantial changes to your work, software for example, you may have to register the new work. Rules vary from jurisdiction to jurisdiction. If you plan to register, seek legal advice before you do so.

TRADE SECRETS

In the information age, information and intellectual property are competitive differentiators. Many jurisdictions have specific trade secret laws. Trade secrets can apply to any sensitive competitive data in your organization. Much of this information is captured in unstructured data like the documents, spreadsheets, and processes commonly used in your organization.

Start protecting your trade secrets by encouraging and enforcing corporate confidentiality with all of your employees. Your employee agreements must make this explicit. IT needs to ensure that proper document controls are in place, including making sure there are no copies of critical trade secret documents that former employees can gain access to.

Cloud-based sharing (e.g., Dropbox) makes it easier for people to collaborate. It also makes it much easier for trade secrets to leave your company and, equally importantly, come into your company from partners, subcontractors, or other third parties without your knowledge.

PORTFOLIO MANAGEMENT

Together, all of your intellectual property is an asset of the company. This asset has to be documented, managed, protected, and enhanced. Protect your intellectual property by viewing it as a portfolio like you would any other asset class. As I shared at the start of this chapter it is easy to take your intellectual property for granted; until such a time as you are facing down competition which is taking advantage of the lack of time and attention given to your intellectual property portfolio. If your company is highly dependent on innovation and trade secrets, you have no choice but to put time and energy into this. In the 21st century every company has to increasingly manage their intellectual property as innovative new ways of doing business are becoming part of every industry.

Case Study:
DOUG BUNKER, FOUNDING SALES PARTNER CLEVEST

For Doug Bunker, the founding sales and marketing leader of Clevest, the third time was indeed the charm. With co-founders Tom Ligocki and Arthur Lo, they set out to transform workforce automation and mobile dispatch for small and mid-sized organizations.

BACKGROUND

MDSI (Mobile Data Solutions Inc, now part of ABB) was a pioneer in creating Advantex, an automated workforce management and dispatch solution that integrated with mobile communication devices suitable for mobile employees. Doug, Tom and Arthur all worked for MDSI. As young technologists and entrepreneurs, they realized that the "big iron" solution MDSI created was suitable for some of the largest telecom and utility companies in the world; it did not scale down to mid-sized organizations in price, functionality, or architecture.

While Doug stayed on at MDSI, Tom and Arthur left MDSI to work for eMobile, a company founded to provide web-based workforce management solutions for the utility industry. Based on their experience with MDSI and eMobile, Tom and Arthur were convinced that modern software architectures coming on stream in the mid-2000s combined with a market focus on smaller organizations was a tremendous market opportunity, so they founded Clevest.

THIRD TIME LUCKY

Doug, Tom and Arthur had worked with Advantex at MDSI. They had also seen how at eMobile a mobile workforce solution could be developed much faster. Thanks to technological changes and experience in anticipating required functionality, features that would take six months at MDSI and one month at eMobile could be developed in one week at Clevest. Key to their innovation strategy was leveraging both their knowledge of workforce management and mobility, along with building and deploying the architecture they created on the most modern software architecture platforms.

Because workforce automation means capturing and implementing business processes and workflows, Arthur and Tom had seen the challenge of quickly and cost effectively implementing these custom workflows for prospects and customers. A second part of their innovation strategy was to create Genesis, their solution to customizing Clevest Mobile Workforce Management (MWFM).

Their original goal was to push the actual customization of the solution to the end customer. They have achieved this goal in a few select cases, but the reality is that even with a lot of training it takes in-depth domain knowledge of both an organization's processes and Clevest's architecture to implement custom rules. Genesis has been a competitive advantage for Clevest—allowing them to implement at a far lower cost than their competitors. They have also been successful in getting some of the third-party vendors in their ecosystem to understand and use Genesis with their customers.

SALES INNOVATION

Because previous workforce automation solutions were big, cumbersome, and required massive amounts of hardware and infrastructure to run, they were very hard to demonstrate in the field. At MDSI, Doug could never give a demonstration of the solution on his own—he always needed to have a sales engineer that lugged around a large trunk containing a Unix server. Not only was this costly, but Doug felt like he was never able to really dig into the prospects' problems then immediately provide feedback to the prospect on product capabilities.

Clevest's use of the best software architectures meant that Doug could load the entire Clevest solution on his laptop, start his own instance of the server, and then show the interplay of the product between a browser window and a mobile device in real-time. This was a game changer in terms of giving the prospect the experience of the solution. They could see the flow of information end-to-end, creating both positive user experiences and belief in their young software company.

This extended to trade shows, where Clevest was one of the few workforce automation vendors that could fully demonstrate their product while at the trade show. Prospects could touch it and feel it creating higher booth traffic and prospect interest, while also positioning Clevest as the technical innovation leader in the space.

COOP UTILITIES

In the early days of Clevest, Doug and Tom focused on local prospects in the region where they were located. These businesses varied from a helicopter repair company to a restoration company that focused on recovery from fires and floods. At MDSI and eMobile, both had spent a lot of time with electric utilities. After chasing large telecom and utility companies without success, they stopped and did an analysis and realized that small to mid-sized Coop Utilities had a need for mobile workforce management solutions. They were more risk tolerant of a smaller supplier, and no one had created a solution they could afford and use.

Unlike their competitors who focused broadly, Doug and Tom realized that they had to make a bet on a single focused vertical to maximize the impact they could have with the few marketing dollars they had. What they discovered is that Coop Utilities have their own trade shows, network, and trade associations. It is a small community and, because they did not compete, everyone talks to everyone else. Once Clevest got some referential customers, they were able to leverage word-of-mouth to help generate further interest. It still took years of effort to get a firm foothold in just this one market.

INTRODUCING AVL

The Clevest vision was a new best-of-breed lower cost complete workforce and mobile scheduling and workflow platform. Selling such a system requires so many changes for a prospect that sales cycles could take years followed by years to integrate with multiple systems. Many of their customers were asking for Automatic Vehicle Location solutions (AVL). AVL uses information from devices installed on vehicles to automatically locate a vehicle and to plot its location on a map. Dispatchers can instantly see exactly where all their vehicles are located and where they are going.

Doug and Tom argued for some time about implementing AVL. Tom viewed it as non-core to the workforce and scheduling and felt other AVL vendors had a head start in the market. Doug argued that the market was asking for this functionality and they were in a perfect position to implement and deploy it as, with minor modifications, AVL functionality was a subset of MWFM. In the end, Clevest invented an AVL solution specifically for the Utility market.

The AVL solution they created was very clever. Coop Utilities had invested hundreds of thousands of dollars in Geographic Information Systems (GIS) with extensive mapping and location information in their markets. Rather than build a mapping interface from scratch, Clevest Automatic Vehicle Location leveraged Coop Utility customers' investment in GIS systems from vendors like ESRI. Prospects and customers saw the maps they were used to, while being able to add a mapping layer with real-time vehicle information. Even long-time skeptical dispatchers, convinced that lists of vehicles were as effective as AVL, became converts after seeing their vehicles on a map in real-time and realizing how much more effective and faster they could be at problem solving and dispatching.

EXPANDING SALES FORCE

For the first several years, Doug personally trained all new account managers. They hired for sales expertise, rather than for industry knowledge of Coop Utilities, workforce management, scheduling, and dispatch. With long sales cycles, it was at least nine months before new account managers had any chance of closing their first sale.

The strategic shift to offering AVL as a product offering had additional benefits to sales. Selling an AVL solution requires far fewer decision makers on the buyer's side and the sales cycle is much faster. This made it easier for new sales people to close their first sales.

For the first years, Clevest was virtually unknown in the conservative Coop Utility market. The AVL solution allowed Clevest to get a foot in the door and had a deployment time of less than a month, demonstrating benefits to customers almost immediately rather than 1-2 years when deploying MWFM. Proving their value with an AVL solution, they were often able to leverage the customer relationship to eventually sell and deploy their full workforce automation solution.

INTERFACE INNOVATION

AVL and workforce management solutions are only as good as the systems they integrate with. Over time, Clevest built interfaces to more and more third-party applications. In some cases, the application vendors would not share interface details. They told Doug that until Clevest had more customers in their installed base, they would not work with them on an interface. These same prospects would not buy from Clevest because they did not have a working interface for their application system, a classic "who goes first" problem.

One of Clevest's partners had built interfaces between Clevest's solutions and some other vendors who were difficult to integrate with. In some cases, the partner had won deals without the permission of the application vendor. In 2012, Clevest realized that the fastest way to gain the innovation and interfaces they needed was to acquire their partner, which is what they did.

DISASTER RECOVERY

Utility and electrical transmission companies face unique challenges in dealing with natural disasters. Whether it is an ice storm in winter or an event such as Hurricane Sandy in the northeast US, the crews of a single Coop or transmission company cannot cope on their own with such natural disasters.

These organizations have emergency plans in place for such events. Crews and equipment are shared between organizations in order to restore infrastructure that has been damaged or destroyed in a natural disaster. Managing all the activity involved is especially difficult as it is outside normal operations and requires the coordination of people from multiple organizations.

While rare, planning and preparation for these events is a core part of every Coop Utility. Clevest modified their AVL solution so that it could quickly be deployed in trucks from other organizations. This provided much greater visibility and operational efficiency for disaster recovery, while once again differentiating Clevest from its competitors. When customers, citizens, and the media are waiting for the electricity to come back on, accurate and timely information about repairs is invaluable. Clevest has since further set itself apart by adding MWFM functionality for outages and storm recoveries.

LESSONS LEARNED

Clevest has seen continuous success and growth since its inception. They have successfully used innovation as a central part of their corporate strategy. The following are key lessons from the approach Doug, Tom, and Arthur took:

1. A short product development time gives you a competitive advantage.

2. You have to commit to a single market segment early in order to differentiate and create market traction.

3. Match market needs, product vision, and innovation to beat your competitors.

4. Accelerate sales by innovating a product solution that can be fully demonstrated at customer sites and trade shows.

Clevest shows us how innovation has to be matched with market focus, products that meet real customer needs, and how innovation can differentiate you in the sales process.

TAKE ACTION NOW

All companies start with some form of innovation. If you want to stay ahead of your competitors, you need to find ways to create new innovations. Motivate and help your employees innovate by recognizing when they create an innovation. Use both industry peers and those outside your industry to breathe new ideas into yourself and your organization. Make conscious choices about your innovation strategy by:

1. Documenting one innovative new idea a person has created in your organization and publicly acknowledge their innovation in the next 30 days.

2. Find five ways your competitors are innovating that you are not.

3. Connect with five experts, inside or outside your industry, before this quarter ends.

MARKETING STRATEGY

It was the summer of 2003 and we had successfully transited the Corinth Canal in Greece. This engineering marvel cut off three hundred nautical miles (five hundred kilometers) of travel between the Ionian and Aegean Seas. After visiting Piraeus and Athens, my goal was to sail Dragonsinger and the family to Istanbul, Turkey. I had dreamed of doing this for much of our trip. To get to Instanbul, we had to sail north.

To be safe, I had used Rod Heikell's Greek Waters Pilot to plan our route and the weather. Rod's book described how in most summers in the Aegean a fierce wind called the *meltimi* blows from the north in the summer. Rod went on to say that the wind starts in June and early July.

I took this to mean that the *meltimi* wouldn't start in early June. Or if it did, it did so only intermittently. We came through the Corinth Canal in late-May and I assumed we would have plenty of time to head north towards Istanbul before the *meltimi* started. As we headed out from Piraeus we were hit with steady winds that measured Force 8 on the Beaufort scale. This scale only goes to 12, and most sailors never go out above Force 7. Almost no one tries to sail against a Force 8.

It was at this point that I admitted to defeat to Karalee. We wouldn't be sailing to Istanbul. After a few days of bashing our way north, we turned around and sailed with the wind. While it continued to blow Force 8, we only put a scrap of sail out and sailed effortlessly and easily down the waves back to Athens and eventually all the way across the Aegean to Turkey.

Marketing strategy is all about finding which way the wind is blowing, predicting how hard it is going to blow, then setting up everything we do to go where the market is going. The *meltimi* has been documented for thousands of years. Few of us are lucky enough to have that sort of insight into where markets are going. There is much we can do to figure out, measure, and adjust our marketing strategy.

VALUE

At Robelle, we had two primary product lines which were priced based on the costs of producing, shipping, and supporting those products. This greatly simplified invoicing, communication, and quoting, which helped

> What is the value to your customers for the problem you solve for them?

us keep costs low. The two product lines delivered dramatically different value to the market. For a long time we never dug into the value we were delivering to the market, underpricing the high value product line. No one ever complained about all the value we were giving away for free. Why would they?

This taught me to look at markets, people, and prospects in terms of the challenge they are facing and the value that a business can deliver in solving that challenge. Price is only one indicator of value.

The monetary value of solving a painful problem for someone is often much lower than the other values you can deliver. These can include reducing risk (that's why we buy insurance), time (there are only 24 hours in a day), convenience, increasing corporate revenue, or increasing productivity (i.e., lowering costs).

In fact, there are only two ways you can deliver value for a business:

1. Increase their revenue, or

2. Lower their costs.

MARKETING CREATES SUCCESS

Most entrepreneurs start a business because they see a need in a market and a have a desire to meet that need. They are opportunistic in their approach, moving from early customer success to the next customer success.

It is rare for entrepreneurs, at least the first time they start a business, to think through and prepare a strategic marketing plan. Most entrepreneurs are ill equipped with the thinking and skills necessary to create a strategic marketing plan. The goal is not a plan, but a deep understanding of the markets you want to go after, what the critical pain points are in those markets, and how you can deliver solutions to customers that truly value solving the pain they are in, letting you make a lot of money in the process. Reg Nordman, Founder of Rocketbuilders, a boutique sales and marketing consulting company, says this about creating your marketing plan:

"It gives entrepreneurs permission to succeed"

SEGMENTATION

Segmentation is breaking your market down into identifiable pieces. We call each piece a segment. Because marketing investment is always limited, we want to find prospects who have similarities and who hang out together. By marketing to each segment as a group, you maximize the return on the marketing investment you make in the segment.

There are many ways to segment a market. Do you sell to customers in your city, state, country, continent, or the world? Using geography is a common way to begin your segmentation. If you sell to businesses, do you focus on those with less than ten, 10-50, or more than 50 employees? Business size is another way to segment your market. If you sell directly to consumers, do you target low, middle, or high-income earners? This is another way you can segment.

VERTICAL FOCUS

It is common to believe you can sell to anyone who can buy and use your product. While this may have been true in the past, prospects today insist that you speak to them in their language, about their problems, and show how you solve those problems in a meaningful way. Create powerful segmenting by using a vertical (i.e., industry) focus.

This requires that your marketing plan and tactics have a laser-like focus on specific industries, organizational size, geography, and many other characteristics. Equally important, you need to focus on the 5-8 key drivers that are affecting that industry. We often believe

> Segment your markets to create powerful plans to market and sell your products and solutions.

that there are 20, 30, 50 or more change drivers in an industry, but the reality is that there are only a handful of trigger events in a given industry that are powerful enough to get people to make a change. Your challenge is to determine which industries you are the best fit for, what are the key change events that are driving that particular industry, and how you and your products fit into making it easy for people who want to change to make the change.

CROSSING THE CHASM

In his classic book, *Crossing the Chasm*, Geoffrey Moore demonstrated how any new technology or idea follows a predictable adoption cycle. You may not be a technology company, but if you are selling a new way of doing things or introducing a new idea to a traditional market, you will follow a similar adoption cycle.

Moore argues that in all markets, there are visionary users who will try anything new. Then, there are early adopters who will try new things once they are easy enough to use. But the majority of the market will not accept a new product or idea (the chasm) until the thought leaders in that marketplace first adopt the solution.

REFERENTIAL CUSTOMERS

If you are introducing a new idea, discover who will be the first custom-ers to purchase your new product or service. As you have initial success, find what is common to those early customers. Then, take a strategic approach to find out who are the thought leaders and influencers in that marketplace. Get them to accept your new idea and you will be on your way to crossing your chasm.

Another key element to market adoption is getting reference customers who will validate your product to other prospects. A mid-size company in the transportation sector is not going to believe the experiences of a person in the retail sector. Building a strategic marketing plan means identifying the market segments you first want to go after, finding out who are the thought leaders in that segment, and getting them to buy and recommend your product, while agreeing to act as a reference to others in the segment.

PAIN POINTS

How do you know if a person is in pain? If you really want to know ask them why three times. The first reason people give you is never the real reason they are considering a change. When you ask why the first time, you

> Discover the really painful problems your prospects need to solve and then solve them.

will get to the first layer of the underlying painful issues that the person, or their boss, is experiencing. By the time you have asked why for the third time, you will be close to the root cause of the problem.

Use these pain points to identify:

1. What segment experiences this pain the most?
2. Who in the organization experiences this pain every day?
3. Is the person with the pain the person that makes the buying decision?

You need the answers to these questions for everything from effective communications to the market to making sure your product or service

WIND IN YOUR SAILS

actually solves the pain you have identified. Build your marketing plan by focusing on the best ways to communicate the challenges and pain people experience. Then, show how your solution eliminates the pain people in the market are experiencing.

BUYER PROCESS

Reg Nordman of Rocketbuilders tells me that he asks every new company that wants to work with him whether they know what their buyers' process is for purchasing products and services like the ones they sell. Only one in fifteen have any notion of what the buying process is for their prospects.

Buying power has shifted from companies to purchasers. There is too much information available today on the Internet for anyone to think they can hide information from buyers. While buyers always had a process, you could get away without knowing it in detail in the past. Today you cannot market and sell without knowing how your prospects buy and what the key drivers are for them to make a change.

Guy Smith, author of *Start-up CEO's Marketing Manual* makes sure the very first thing he does when working with a new company is to itemize every stakeholder who has any degree of influence over the purchase process. This includes people who have functional veto power. They may not have organizational veto power but they can stop a project if they decide to. For example, in technology companies the techies have a tremendous amount of veto power. They can park their butts on the ground and stop multi-million dollar projects from ever starting.

After itemizing everyone in the buying process, Guy then finds out where in the sales cycle these people should be brought in. Bringing people in too early can have adverse effects. Next, you should document what you need to communicate to each stakeholder at each point in the sales process. The goal behind this is not only mapping their motivation so that you can address their concerns correctly, but also anticipating any objections so you can knock those out of the way quickly. The overall effect is to shrink the sales cycle tremendously. It is stunning how few companies actually take the time to fully understand the buying process from the buyer's point of view.

POSITIONING

All companies, products, and services operate in a market. How these are perceived is your position in the market. Marketing is an effective way to impact your perceived and real position in the marketplace. It is impossible to position in a vacuum. Human beings automatically rate you relative to something else. Your positioning is a function of how you provide similarities and contrasts to other companies and products in the markets where you operate.

When positioning, start with the pain points you have identified in your market segments. Focus on the needs of your markets and prospects. Everyone has wants, but they will only pay you to solve true needs that only you can look after. The bigger their pain and the more effective your pain pill, the more value you deliver to your markets and customers.

CORPORATE POSITIONING

We often mix up our company with our products. Your company has unique characteristics and values. Corporate positioning begins with what makes your company unique. All of your communications, marketing materials, training, and sales must highlight those three or four things that make your company different from all the others. Remember that if you have a strong track record of success, one thing that makes you different is that your success reduces the risk of prospects who want to do business with you. This can be powerful positioning when combined with compelling customer stories.

PRODUCT POSITIONING

Focus your product positioning on the specific pain points your prospects experience and how you provide the best solution to these specific challenges. This is where a vertical focus provides an advantage, because you can position your product relative to the biggest challenge of the market you are going after. If all you compete on is a feature-by-feature comparison with your competitors, you will be in a race to the lowest price. By focusing on the value you create for your customers—either lower costs or higher sales—you will stay true to the deep problems they need solved by buying and using your product. Great products and positioning can completely eliminate your competitors.

IDEAL CUSTOMER

Most businesses start out opportunistically, getting whatever customers they can to start with. Once they have acquired customers, they are loath to let them go. The truth is that all customers are not created equal. There is an ideal customer for your products and services. The challenge is figuring out the characteristics of those key customers.

> Fire those customers that are not aligned with your core values and ideal customer profile.

A starting point to figuring this out is to focus on your corporate strategy by looking at your core values. Are the customers you have aligned with your core values? As you grow and develop as an entrepreneur and a company, you will deepen your core values. At some point, you will discover that you need to only go after and retain customers that align with your values. It may seem hard to let some customers go, but keeping the right ones eliminates massive headaches and lets your organization focus on what it does best. The result will be even more of the customers you want.

COMMUNICATION

With your markets clearly defined, knowledge of the key pain points in each of your vertical markets, and product solutions that do a great job of solving these pain points, you are ready to communicate to your markets. This is a key role of marketing—to communicate your company and its products in the best possible light in your company's key markets.

It is critical that all your communications be from the point of view of the market. All too often I listen to entrepreneurs tell the world how wonderful they are and that self belief and passion will take you far. Speaking from the point of view of who you are selling to will take you much further.

Use the language and pain points of your markets to set the story for all of your marketing materials. Show how people have used your products and services to solve these pain points for them. Get customers to provide testimonials, case studies, and video examples you can use. A customer talking about their experience with you is worth ten times that which you write or say about yourself.

CHANNELS

Our 21st century world has a lot of communication channels. You need to find the ones your markets are listening to. Many traditional methods are valid today, including trade shows, face-to-face meetings, webinars, and trade publications.

While almost all trade publications have electronic editions, they are no less valuable. Prospects trust the editors of those trade publications to make judgments they can rely on. By being strategic in your markets, you should be able to identify the two or three top editors. Share information with these editors, be available to be the trusted expert that they quote, and pre-release information to them on a rotating basis. Every editor needs good content.

When it comes to providing information to customers they have preferences for whether they like to push or pull the information they want. For example, I often prefer to receive information by email. I want you to push your information directly into my inbox. It is a more convenient method for me.

Other people prefer to pull information. Publishing a blog lets people pull information from it by viewing the postings. Some readers may in fact receive your blog in pull mode by reading the postings via RSS or by hearing about them in one of your push communication channels (e.g., email, Facebook, or Twitter).

The key is to be aware of your customer preferences. Some people may even prefer the old fashioned way—via ink on paper delivered to their physical place of business. Work on discovering what your market and channels prefer and then deliver the right content at the right time the way your prospects and customers want to receive information.

STORIES THAT CREATE BUZZ

Can you remember when you were young and thought about meeting friends at the amusement park? The sense of anticipation, the excitement, and finally meeting up with your friends and taking your first ride together; feeling the buzz of friendship, adrenaline, and a night out.

I recall a client I was working with doing customer interviews about how their products and services were used. As I listened to example after example of the tremendous value that my client's firm delivered to customers, I felt this same buzz. I could feel the hair on the back of my neck stand up as I sensed how powerfully my client's customers were using their solution.

All too often, a customer's sense of excitement gets lost in the overwhelming noise we are subjected to every day. When you market yourself, you need to create that sense of buzz your best customers already have about you. They believe. You need to believe. Then, the world needs to believe.

People love a great story. Having excited customers makes it easy to tell believable stories, because the proof points are already there. Tell stories that create buzz.

CONSISTENCY OF BRAND

In Corporate Strategy, I wrote about your Brand Promise—the #1 measurable promise that you make to your markets. Our goal in marketing is to create a consistent customer experience that leads people to have an emotional response to our company, brand promise, products, and services. Every touch point you have between people in

> **BRAND PROMISE**
> The #1 measurable promise that you make to your markets.

your company and people outside your company is an opportunity to enhance or detract from that customer experience and brand promise.

The goal of a branding style guide is to create a consistent look and feel of everything that a company communicates. As individuals, we respond to much more than the just the words we read or hear. We engage with all of our senses, reacting to colors, fonts, packaging, sound, and more.

Creating a consistent brand presence is a big challenge. In many cases, marketing materials are created over time, by different people, with no thought to consistency. Many are not even aware they are creating branding elements. The technical person who sets up an email account for a new employee has never been trained to show how configuring the font, font size, and signature is an important piece of the corporate branding mosaic.

The easiest way to create brand consistency and experience is by creating and using a corporate style guide. This becomes the master document that everyone refers to. Training, education, and processes are needed to make it easy for everyone in an organization to follow style and branding guidelines.

Isabelle Mercier-Turcotte, co-founder of LeapZone Strategies provides these reasons for creating and using a style guide in the blog post Here Is Why A Style Guide Is "Crucial" To Building A Thriving Brand:[3]

Maintaining consistent communication brings:

- Ease of decision-making
- A common flow among the team
- A clear sense of direction
- A uniform customer experience

SOCIAL MEDIA

There is a gold rush mentality to social media—everyone feels like they need to do it. If the majority of the decision makers in your market are over

3   www.leapzonestrategies.com/blog/2009/12/here-is-why-a-style-guide-is-crucial-to-building-a-thriving-brand/

fifty, do they even look at social media? Social media can be a powerful tool in your communications mix, but it needs to be prioritized, just like all of your other channels. Social media works best with small tidbits of information, rather than long articles. To keep up a steady stream of news, it often makes sense to hire a third-party to take your regular news and then be proactive about repackaging and sharing it on social media.

Blogging can be an effective way to establish yourself as a thought leader. Doing so requires a sustained effort over a long period of time. If you are going to start blogging, consider these best practices:

1. Establish a schedule and stick to it, whether it is three times a week or once a month.

2. Promote new blog posts across as many of your communication channels as possible.

3. Encourage and support commentary on your blog posts.

4. Guest blog on influential blogs in your markets.

5. Get others to be guests and write posts for your blog.

6. Feature customer stories and successes. Like all communications, it should be about your markets and customers, not about you.

7. If you blog about an event, make sure that your blog post is very close in time to the completion of the event (e.g., within 2-3 days after the close of a trade show).

EMAIL NEWSLETTERS

Email can be a powerful way to communicate. The challenge is that all of us are so inundated with email that it is easy for you to be lost in the clutter. A regular newsletter containing relevant information can make it easy for you to stay in touch with your customers and prospects. Focus on these best practices to ensure that your email newsletters are effective:

1. Only send as often as your readers are willing to tolerate. Monitor the unsubscribe rate to see if you are sending too often.

2. Keep to a regular schedule and do not deviate from that schedule.

3. Use a proven template that showcases your branding.

4. Make sure your email template works across a wide range of email clients, including all current mobile devices and email apps.

5. Measure open and click through rates to see how engaged your audience is with your content.

6. Use a third-party delivery service (e.g., MailChimp, Constant Contact, or Campaign Monitor to name a few).

TRADITIONAL MEDIA

In the rush to the electronic frontier, people are often leaving behind traditional media. If your market appreciates 3D flyovers of your designs and you can cost effectively provide those, do so. If your buyers need a high quality brochure in their hands to create belief in your company and products, give them one. You should not be deciding what the market needs—the market, via your market research, should be telling you what the market needs to be convinced you are a trustworthy and believable vendor to do business with.

I have personally experienced the value of traditional printed media. A few years ago, Karalee and I were planning a spring break vacation with our daughter Jocelyn and son Allen. The physical presence of the brochure in the travel agency lent credence to the idea of the holiday we were planning. At least for travel, brochures, which are packaged as booklets, continue to have more of an impact than their online counterparts for these reasons:

1. There are hundreds of photographs in the booklet. You can scan these photographs in a fraction of the time it would take you to look at the same number online.

2. You can flip through the booklet quickly, pausing at anything that catches your attention. If you know exactly where you want to go, online resources can zero in on the specific choices. If you just want a general style of holiday (sun, Europe, adventure ...) a booklet focused on the style that interests you provides many more possibilities.

3. Fast price comparisons. The booklet we looked at had prices on every single page. You can quickly see the tradeoffs of different price points, in either location or quality.

The consistent layout of the booklet made comparisons far easier for one vacation choice to another. The entire booklet was organized by location. Each vacation choice was laid out in the same manner, using the same type fonts, colors, and keywords.

Beyond these practical features of a booklet, there is an even more important marketing reason why they work. Humans are tactile beings. The more we can feel and touch something, the more real it seems to us. The booklets we looked at were hefty. They felt substantial. The booklet we finally chose from was over 170 pages long. The booklets are beautifully laid out and printed on semi-gloss paper. It all adds up to creating belief that the vendor can deliver a great vacation for our family. And, for the record, that piece of marketing material was the deciding factor for us spending a week on a Sunquest vacation in Puerto Vallarta.

DELIVER EVENTS AND PRODUCTS

Once you have thought through your marketing strategy, marketing implementation revolves around two deliverables:

1. Events
2. Products

Events include trade shows, webinars, road shows, networking and more. The type and scale of each event determines the amount of effort to be put into it. All events have a process associated with them. The key is making sure that you decide and track all the events for the year and the processes that go with them.

A brochure, stand, demo, tweet, blog post, or article are all examples of work products that marketing produces. By treating these marketing artifacts as products, you can manage them as you would any product—there is a start, a middle, and an end—another process.

MARKETING CALENDAR

No matter the size of the organization, a lot of time and effort are required to keep track of all the marketing communications, events, and deliverables. To realize the power of all of your marketing efforts you must coordinate all your marketing activities. One of the best ways I have found to lay out these activities and coordinate them is with a marketing calendar.

> Use a centralized marketing calendar to coordinate everyone's activities.

When I work with organizations I get them to put all of their planned marketing activities on a calendar. People are often surprised at how many activities they are doing, how much overlap there is and where the big gaps are in the schedule.

If there is no suitable calendar software, I recommend you use a spreadsheet to record all the activities. Whatever tool you are using, use this process to create the calendar:

- Write down every month of the year.
- For every month beyond the current quarter, record major events. This should include trade shows, major announcements, product releases, industry events, and anything else relevant to your markets and company.
- For the current quarter, create an entry for each week.
- For each week, write down each of the events for each day. Be sure to include the internal tasks that must be completed for an external event.
- Highlight the external events in a different color from the internal tasks that must be completed.

Case Study:
JAMES SHAW, FOUNDER TWIN CREEK MEDIA

Founded in 2004 by James Shaw, Twin Creek Media started out as digital media experts creating web sites for companies. Their initial marketing and sales efforts were anything but digital. A breakthrough moment, however, forced them to rethink their strategy to move in a new direction.

BACKGROUND

Early in his career James bounced from social work, to computer graphics, to a one-year stint selling financial products for Sun Life. That job convinced him that he didn't want to do sales for a living. Still feeling unfulfilled, James decided to utilize some computer skills he had developed at an engineering job and moved into digital media.

He enrolled in a two-year digital marketing program in Kelowna, BC where he lived. While there, he and a couple of other students started selling their digital media skills and gaining their first clients, creating Twin Creek Media.

SUPPORTING A FAMILY

When James graduated he had a wife and two kids to look after and a mortgage to pay, needing twice as much as the $10/hour jobs he was offered in order to support his family. With no choice left, James decided that he had to make Twin Creek Media a success. Time to do sales again!

While his skills and services were focused almost exclusively on digital media, he found that the only way to build the business was to find customers the traditional way. With almost no marketing budget, James put his time and effort into one-on-one networking and presentations to his local market. Over a two-year period, he attended at least three networking events per week, selling Twin Creek Media's services.

With his experience at Sun Life, James knew that it was a numbers game. If he got out there, spoke with enough people, followed up, and asked for the business he would get it. While it was a brutal process, James made

Twin Creek Media a success, supporting his family, which included the addition of a son in 2006.

CHANGE IN STRATEGY

While Twin Creek Media started out as a specialist marketing company offering web development and digital services, by 2010 they realized that the market was changing. All the other firms offering marketing services were specializing—either into specific vertical segments like real estate or into specific services like search engine optimization or web development.

What no one was doing was becoming an integrated marketing company that could be a one-stop shop where a company could get all the marketing services they needed. While marketing strategy suggests you should segment, sub-segment, and then segment again, this approach went against this common wisdom. Unless you view the market as those companies and organizations that crave a single vendor to work with to service all their marketing needs.

James built his executive team, adding two new partners. At the same time they created an extended virtual network of subcontractors who could provide a wide variety of specialized services. The partners would meet with clients to establish the strategy and then facilitate and manage the projects needed to execute the strategy. Twin Creek Media were the only company in their market, and still are today, to offer the full range of strategic, planning, and implementation services in the Kelowna market.

IDEAL CUSTOMER

James' strategy was to be careful to not be everything to everyone. While they decided to become generalists, they kept their focus on ideal clients. These are small to medium-sized businesses of 10 to 50 employees. In the Kelowna area, there are many such businesses, especially owner-operated ones. They also look for entrepreneurs who:

- Have built a successful business with significant revenue
- Are driven
- Want to continue growing

- Have a strong feeling of pride in what they have built
- Know that changes have been coming for the last ten years

James and his partners usually sell to the owner, although they often work closely with a marketing director or team. They start with an initial meeting and a discovery Q&A document, then produce a 15-page proposal, project budget, and timeline. Typically, initial projects are 2-4 months long and cost $5,000 - $25,000. About 50% of clients do follow on projects.

James' goal is to be a "Plug 'N Play" outsourced marketing department. About 60% of their customers are in BC, with some in Alberta, others across Canada, and a few international. Because James and his partners keep their customers focused on manageable short-term projects, they are able to quickly create value for their customers, showing them the value of marketing, branding, and lead generation.

COMMUNICATION MISMATCH

James sees big marketing challenges for small and medium-sized companies today. They are successful. While they have built a sustainable business, they have been so busy that they have not been aware of the changes going on around them, especially those that involve how people find them and the first impression people get from a company's web site. Bad customer experiences, especially online, are now hurting good companies.

Newspaper and print advertising continue to take the biggest hit. Prospects now have hundreds of options, not five or six, to find business services. The technology, especially for web sites and mobile, has come so far, so fast, that most clients are out of their depth.

BRAND

James says that many of his clients have millions of dollars in top line revenue, yet their web site looks like a child created it. There is a gap between how customers perceive the business and how someone who doesn't know the business views it through the lens of their web site.

This extends beyond just web sites and online presence to their overall branding. Many of Twin Creek Media's clients have built powerful brands over the years. Because of their success, branding has been ignored for a long time so that clients need a brand refresh, including all their traditional marketing materials. As a full service firm, Twin Creek Media focuses on the overall goals for a business and then works with their clients to come up with the best branding and implementation plan.

SEARCH

The way a prospect finds a business has changed. Many people, especially well-off middle-aged people, continue to move to Kelowna. They need everything from used cars to local coffee shops. When those people search for the business services they need they will most likely do the search on a mobile device.

Does your existing web site look okay and is it usable on a mobile device? James asserts that any web site built five or more years ago is virtually unusable on a mobile device today, yet 25% of all traffic is from mobile devices. Today, your web site must work on both desktops and mobile devices.

SPEED

As the Internet continues to grow and all of us change our behaviors to take advantage of new technology from search engines to smart phones, businesses need to change with us. This change is accelerating—who remembers the yellow pages? Old ways of thinking don't work in the Internet age.

James asserts that one Internet year equals twenty-five human years. Way back in 2010 was 100 years ago in Internet time. James says that business owners are coming to the realization that this speed of change is for real. They have known for some time that they have to invest in their marketing, but more are realizing that they need to do it now. There is accelerating belief by owners that they are behind.

LIVING THEIR STRATEGY

Successful marketing firms can themselves often fall behind in their branding and marketing presence. This can create a disconnect for potential clients who want the confidence of a 21st century full-service marketing company. In a noisy world, James communicates across numerous channels to demonstrate his company's skills and to connect with prospects.

James and his team have invested a lot of time and energy in their own branding. The Twin Creek Media web site uses the latest in design techniques, showing up beautifully in both browsers and mobile devices. James was an early blogger. He continues to write extensively on the changing landscape of today's marketing world. He shares best practices across both online and traditional media. He regularly connects to his network via an email newsletter. Client testimonials and success stories fill both their web site and blog, creating belief in their prospects and customers that Twin Creek Media can and does create success for their clients.

ENGAGEMENT

James and his team work towards engagement across all communication channels. While newspapers are on the decline, there is still a place for newspaper advertising. Radio advertising can still be effective. James asserts that "when done right, advertising doesn't feel like advertising, it feels like entertainment or conversation or something else that we enjoy."

By taking a full strategic perspective, Twin Creek Media is able to create brands, ads, web sites, social media campaigns, powerful stories, and communications that bring people in to engage with the businesses they help. James says, "any media channel should be investigated for its appropriateness to the industry, audience and communications goal. In the end, ignoring any of them, whether traditional or digital is a mistake".

FAIL EARLY, FAIL OFTEN

From those early days when James was scrambling to earn a living for his young family to the success that he enjoys today, he notes one consistent experience in his entrepreneurial journey. He has failed. Over and over again he has seen failure, picked himself up, and then pushed ahead.

James says, "Assume that you will fail. Get over it. Starting Twin Creek Media is the hardest thing I have ever done in my entire life. I don't dwell on the failures. I learn from them and move on to the next thing, adapting quickly as I learn from what doesn't work. Make sure that you have a support group of friends and your family to lift you up in those inevitable periods where you have to overcome the challenges of the business."

LESSONS LEARNED

James started with the realization that taking his analytical, sales, and social skills and putting them together would be fun. Having to support a young family, he felt that the only viable option was to create his own business. Through good times and bad he has persevered so that Twin Creek Media is itself a trusted brand that delivers what companies need from their marketing efforts. Key thoughts from James' experience include:

1. Be prepared to put in the effort needed to get your brand out there, asking for business, from the outset.

2. Know who your ideal customer is and the value that you bring to people like them.

3. Use marketing strategy to differentiate your company from your competitors, even if this takes you in a dramatically new direction.

4. Powerful communication, across numerous channels, creates belief and awareness for a company and its brand.

5. Expect to fail, learn from each failure, and move on to your next challenge and success.

6. Hire "can-do" people that are better than you at something.

Twin Creek Media are experts at marketing strategy and the revenue generating capability it provides to business owners. They also believe in what they sell, using the same marketing strategy to make Twin Creek Media a success.

TAKE ACTION NOW

Highly profitable companies make bold marketing promises and then deliver on them. You must document and measure yourself on your brand promise every day. Your product or service is only of value to a select number of people. Focusing your energies on only these people will create spectacular results.

Marketing teams should be held accountable for the same deadlines and deliverables (events and products) as other parts of your company. Challenge your marketing by making sure that you can answer these questions today:

1. What is your measurable brand promise?

2. What are your key markets and who are the key referential customers in each of them?

3. Do you know your critical marketing deadlines for the next six months?

SALES STRATEGY

In the two years we sailed the Mediterranean with our family we often felt like pioneers forging new routes across the vast Mediterranean Sea. For thousands of years mariners have been plying these waters. Every time I thought we were being original, I would learn that the obvious points I was plotting for our routes were exactly the same ones the Phoenicians, Greeks, Romans, and Venetians had used.

No doubt, hundreds of thousands of individuals over the centuries followed exactly the same routes that we did. While the experience felt new and exciting to us, in many ways it was our routes and experience were predictable.

Selling is the same. There are only a handful of ways to sell products. While you may feel that you are breaking new territory with your sales efforts, the truth is that others have gone before you. The trick is to find those methods that have worked for others and then follow their path. The difference for you is to make sure that you measure progress along each sales path you follow, adjusting course as you find which ones work and which ones don't.

DEFINING A SALES MODEL

When Bob and Annabelle started Robelle they rented their first software product, Qedit. Their goal was to have twenty-six people renting Qedit and then live off that income. While Robelle was started only a year or two after the successful launch of the HP3000, the market was already defining how software products were sold. The model was a perpetual license with an accompanying maintenance contract, typically for 20% of the license fee of the product.

Bob and Annabelle adjusted to this model, giving up the rental model, and coming up with a license price for Qedit and fees for maintenance. Sales were direct in the US and Canada and all sales were done over the telephone. The model was "try before you buy." Prospects were sent a tape with a 30-day version of the software. We learned early on that prospects said they would try the software within the 30 days. The reality was that prospects would get distracted fighting fires and often wouldn't get around to trying the software until it had already expired.

Today, we don't have the luxury of time. Buyers, more than ever, control the purchasing process. You have to figure out your sales channel, sales process, and measure it for success.

SALES CHANNELS

Buyers have preferences about how they purchase products and services and who they buy them from. For each of your markets you need to have sales channels that align with how your buyers want to purchase. If they will only buy face-to-face, you have to build a direct sales force. To gain trust, you may need to use partner channels to gain access to your markets.

Each sales channel has its own communication, management, and measurement challenges. Many entrepreneurs think that once they have signed up a large partner, all of their sales challenges are over. You will find that keeping top of mind awareness through any major partner is as difficult as keeping top of mind awareness in markets you are approaching directly.

Focus your energies on what makes the channel successful, whether direct or indirect. Partners will only perform well when it is easy for them to engage, quote, close, and fulfill orders for your products. Your own sales force may be able to put up with complications in the sales process, but it will restrict your revenue growth. Make it easy for your prospects to buy and for partners and sales people to sell.

BUYER PROCESS

The world has moved to a buying process—the buyers have more information and more control than ever. Buyers are entering the sales cycle much later in the process. Mark Stuyt trains global organizations in this seismic shift in buying patterns. He estimates the entry point into the sales funnel for prospects is now 60-65% into the entire buying process. The sales person no longer gets to educate and recommend. Prospects are principally validating their research.

> You must match your sales process to how your prospects buy and not the other way round.

Many entrepreneurs I have interviewed for this book say that today's B2B sales people must have a challenger mentality. They must be prepared to ask the prospect why they are willing to make a change. It is no longer about features and benefits. It is about how purchasing a product or service and making a change in organizational processes can result in better outcomes. Those better outcomes must be defined in terms of the prospect's own business.

QUALIFYING

Because buyers engage with businesses much later in the sales process, it is critical that sales people be capable of challenging prospects' assumptions and being skilled at:

- Understanding the qualifying process
- Making sure that sales people do not rush through this part of the sales process
- Stop making assumptions about the prospect
- Keep checking assumptions all the way along

- Ask the question "does the person you are talking to have the authority to make the purchasing decision?"

EXPERTISE VERSUS EXPERIENCE

Colin Parker spends his life training and developing sales professionals as the founder of Lone Star Sales Performance. He says, "We often confuse expertise with experience. If a person has been selling with the same company for fifteen years, they have a lot of experience. They have expertise in that market and in selling the company's products. That does not translate into expertise, especially if the sales professional changes company, markets, and products."

In developing sales professionals, you must have a process with objective measures of expertise. Give pay increases for a demonstrated increase in ability and not for more time (i.e., experience) on the job. Develop formalized sales training, feedback, and measures in order to make this successful.

As you grow and expand your company into new markets and products, you must put the time and effort into further training and measures for your sales force. Just because an individual has been successful in your original market, do not assume they will automatically be successful in a new market. The new market will likely have different pain points and processes.

Your sales people will not tell you when they are in over their heads. We hire sales people because they are confident and believe in themselves. This can be a curse when a sales person is in a situation that is beyond their capacity and understanding. They will almost never admit they are lost.

LISTENING IN

Colin and I are major proponents of listening in on sales calls. These conversations tell you a lot about all aspects of your sales process, training, and an individual's confidence and knowledge level. You can do this by asking your sales people to silently conference you in on telephone calls. For face-to-face meetings, sales leaders must accompany sales people on prospect visits on a regular basis. You can also get your sales people to record calls, but they need to inform their prospects that they are being recorded.

Do your sales people record and listen to their own sales calls on a regular basis? All of us have felt self conscious when listening to ourselves. We often need coaching help to force us to listen to our own mistakes. If we don't listen in on our own calls, how will we ever improve? A combination of you listening in and providing feedback combined with self-listening is a powerful path to improved sales performance.

KNOW YOUR SALES PROCESS

Many businesses start with the entrepreneur doing all of the initial sales. Geof Auchinleck, co-founder and CEO of Neoteric says this about his partner Lyn Sharman: "I was so fortunate to have a partner who lived to sell. I would come up with products and Lyn knew and loved to sell it."

> You can only scale your business when you have a repeatable sales process.

While passionate about their business and products, a business can only scale so much if only one person is doing all of the selling. Geof was indeed fortunate to have a partner like Lyn. At some point a business needs to hire a sales person and develop a sales process. To be successful your sales process needs to:

- Fit with your market's buying process.
- Be focused on closing sales for people who are ready to buy.
- Have measurable activities.
- Clearly define how a sales person moves a prospect through the sales process.

Of the fifty companies Reg Nordman of Rocketbuilders has trained in building a formalized marketing and sales plan, none of them had a sales process. Half of the companies Rocketbuilders have helped had a Customer Relationship Management System (CRM). Companies think that the CRM they buy instituted a formal process but the reality is that

CRM systems only implement a formal sales process if you create and document one.

If you are an entrepreneur who has been the primary sales person, take the time to step back from all of your roles to clearly document how you sell. You will have a process that you followed, although you might need a facilitator to pull that process out of you. If you already have a sales team, but no formal sales process, put your best sales people in a room and then get them to document each of the key success factors that leads to them closing sales. A facilitator can help to separate key activities that advance the sales process from all of the myriad tasks a sales professional does.

Whether starting from scratch or improving on your existing processes, high performing organizations have a documented sales process. You also need to put in the key measurements that let you know that your sales people are moving through the sales process successfully.

FUNNEL MANAGEMENT

Garry Rasmussen built ISM-BC into a $500M revenue company before retiring to become an angel investor and director of numerous high growth technology companies. Through many different companies, markets, and products, he has built an outline of what he looks for as key stages of the sales funnel in B2B markets:

25%   Customer has an identified problem that they have budget to solve.

50%   Approval to proceed. Funds allocated.
Company confirmed as still in the running.

75%   Verbal agreement that the company has won.

90%   Agreement on terms, especially on limitations of liability.

As Chairman of the board, Garry still insists on funnel reviews at least once a quarter. As a successful entrepreneur, Garry makes sure that he digs into the details of the funnel before being convinced that the numbers are true.

ACTIVITY NOT OUTCOMES

A closed sale is a result of many small steps. We tend to focus on the outcome—revenue, when we only have control over the actions that our sales people perform—activities. You need to define your own percentages in the sales process and the key gate keeper activities that must be completed for a sales person to be successful.

> Manage sales by managing the activities your sales people do.

For example, assume that to close a sale a sales person needs to have fifteen conversations. Not email threads, but actual person-to-person conversations either in person or over the phone. By measuring the number of conversations that every sales person has every day, you can know whether you are on track or not.

Activities should be measured from the buyer's perspective. Many people count the number of quotes sent. If the quotes are being sent to the wrong person, not being reviewed, or if there is no feedback on the quote, the act of sending the quote does nothing to advance the sales process.

PRESENTING PROPOSALS

In this day and age we assume that everything is done by email. While email has its use, it is a terrible tool in sales for gauging buyer feedback. Insist that all proposals be done either face-to-face or over the telephone in a booked meeting.

If meeting face-to-face, hand out the proposal just before your proposal meeting starts. For phone presentations, send the proposal just as everyone joins the meeting on the phone. The presentation should be scripted and follow these steps:

1. Remind the prospect of the pain they are in.

2. Show them a vision of a future state where by working with you they can solve the pain they are in.

3. Provide the investment decision they need to make to get to the future state they desire.

4. Ask for the close.

This assumes that you have all the key decision makers (see Buyer Process) viewing and responding to the proposal presentation. Even by telephone, you can get a sense of how your audience is taking the proposal, plus, you are there to immediately answer any short-term questions that come up.

When sending a proposal by email, you do not have the opportunity to gain a feel for people's reactions. You also cannot be certain that all key stakeholders in the buying process have seen or approved your proposal.

Case Study:
VIK KHANNA, FOUNDER OF FARONICS

"It doesn't matter what size or business you're in—when you're starting your sales and marketing should never be separated."
—Vik Khanna, Founder of Faronics

You can't have a business unless you learn how to sell. Faronics has become the leader in making computers used in education safe for students to use. This is the story of how four partners came together to solve a real need, building Faronics into a multi-million dollar software company by selling their product, Deep Freeze.

BACKGROUND

Faronics started in 1996 as a computer hardware import/export business which then became a white box computer manufacturer and computer parts wholesaler. It was a low margin, high cash, and inventory intensive business in which a significant amount of business was done with local school districts. One of Vik's local customers was a software company that also bought his hardware. A friendship developed and in July 1999 they asked Vik if he could introduce them to some school district clients when they launched Deep Freeze. Vik immediately asked for the rights to sell this product, seeing it as a high margin and low inventory product line. This turned out to be a wise decision as he ended up having an incredibly successful 18 years with Faronics and Deep Freeze.

Deep Freeze addressed a critical need in education. Computers were increasingly being used as part of the teaching curriculum. As students used these computers, they became corrupted with computer viruses and other malware that made them inoperable. Rather than teaching on the computers, teachers were spending much of their time administering the computers.

The breakthrough was the creation of a way to take a snapshot of a clean version of an operating system and then recreate that snapshot at every reboot. Deep Freeze was the resulting product. Deep Freeze and other follow-on products are today licensed on eight million computers in 150 countries around the world.

INITIAL SALES

Early on in Faronics' history, during some of their most rapid growth, they had no marketing department per se. It was just one continuous ball without any differentiation—it was designed to be that way. Vik was one of the main sales people in the early days.

Faronics' target market was all of the US and Canada. Rather than implementing a vertical territory strategy (e.g., West, Central, and East) they broke down the territories into geographic strips that ran horizontally across the US. Each sales person would be given equal opportunity across all three US time zones, based on population. That way, every sales person was on an equal playing field in terms of time zones and population. This created a sense of competition amongst the sales team. As one of the sales people, Vik applied the same rules and commissions to himself as to all the other sales people.

Faronics based their selling model on try before you buy. Not only does this support their personal selling, marketing, and product management style, they believe that if prospects can try something before buying it, the prospects will create their own beliefs about the product. At Faronics, the sales person's job is to facilitate, not to actually sell prospects.

TRADE SHOWS

At first, Vik personally did 35 trade shows in one year as he was growing the business. He used to drive from Oklahoma to Texas, from trade show to trade show, carrying the Faronics banner with him. He would set it up, work the show, break it down, and then drive to the next city to do it all over again.

As Faronics grew, Vik noted that certain issues that used to come up back in those early days were still problems, including managing trade shows. "If you are a sales person and have a trade show in your territory you are going to go there." Vik's experience was that the impact of a sales person going to a trade show as a sales person has ten times the returns of sending a marketing person to a trade show on the sales team's behalf.

They always had a rule at Faronics—if you're going out travelling, don't make it just for the trade show. Spend at least one extra day visiting customers or prospects. This allows you to maximize your time and learn directly face-to-face with people. Also, when you're at the trade show, are there any sessions you can attend? Is there any thought leadership you can do? These ideas are as important today as ever. Trade shows are not just about standing around a booth hoping people will come by. Be proactive and maximize your time out of the office.

MARKETING VERSUS SALES

Vik believes that prospecting is a sales job that's also a marketing job. He often found that the sales person would sit there doing nothing because the marketing department hadn't got the leads. Sales people can cold call, so the challenge was how to make a sales person hungrier? How do you make that inception point between marketing and sales more synergistic?

Vik strived to create a sales team that was competitive yet cooperative. With a competitive sales team, each sales person is running their own territories, their own business in their territories, and each individual needs to do prospecting to get their own leads. Whether they get these leads from marketing or from cold calls doesn't matter. There was a "gold rush mentality" where Vik challenged each sales person to figure out how they could get the maximum revenue out of their individual sales territory, saying that "From my experience at Faronics, this was pivotal. If we had set up at the beginning both a sales team and a marketing team we would not have got the results; we would have got a certain factor but not the ten times that we got in that hungry gold rush culture."

MANAGING SALES PEOPLE

From the early days onward, Vik and his sales managers collected weekly statistics from their sales people. He points out that not all calls are of the same quality. They track calls that are longer than 30 seconds. In his experience, you get a much better picture of what is going on when you are tracking longer calls.

For sales management there are ways to hold your account managers accountable and execute on your game plan. At the end of the day, no one likes to do all the hard work of cold calls, so you must actively manage your sales people. Vik has seen it over and over again, where sales people are sitting there waiting while the leads are coming, but they do not believe that the leads are coming in fast enough. The issue is not the quantity of the leads, but the quality.

The best sales people Vik has ever found are the ones that have a bent towards product management; a sales person that can truly dig into the real problem a prospect has and why they are not buying. Finding out why a person is not buying and then addressing that by taking the issue back to the team puts the solution on the product road map. Great sales people then go back to the customer, it can even be a year later, saying, "A year ago I contacted you and you said you're not going to buy it because it doesn't have feature x. You know what, it's been a year later and we've added feature x to our new product that just been released. You can try it today." Not only is that person going to be so happy that you listened to them properly and you got back to them, but now they're going to give you their consideration because they told you that if you put feature x in they're going to buy it.

GLOBAL EXPANSION

International expansion came through channel partners. Initially, some proactive entrepreneurs reached out and inquired about whether Faronics had a reseller program. They quickly created one and still have ongoing relationships with the initial partners that contacted them in 2000 and 2001 from the United Kingdom, Denmark and Australia.

Faronics, under the leadership of Vik's partner, Farid Ali, got proactive about recruiting partners in many countries and opened an international office in London followed by another office in Singapore. Today, via over 100 channel partners, Faronics sells in over 60 countries. Interestingly, the model that Vik used in direct selling was shared with all Faronics' partners and in some countries it worked well. In countries where relationship selling is the norm, which is most countries, cold calling was ineffective and partners had to use the selling style that worked best in their markets.

LESSONS LEARNED

Four partners, each with their own expertise, came together, saw a market need and then developed an industry-leading product to address that need. Among the lessons learned:

1. Hire sales people who can really dig into the needs of prospects—looking beyond the first one or two objections to dig into the real problem the prospect faces.
2. Create a structure that makes sales people hungry, monitoring and managing them on an individual basis.
3. It is the calls longer than 30 seconds that really count in sales.
4. Teamwork between sales, marketing, and product management has the greatest impact on future sales.

While four partners came together to form Faronics, Vik was the sales leader that took to the road to sell Deep Freeze and who hired and created the sales culture that led to their success. During the process, Vik held himself accountable to the same measures that he held all the other sales people accountable to. The proof of Vik's strategy is in the worldwide success that Faronics has achieved.

TAKE ACTION NOW

We put an extraordinary amount of effort and worry into the outcome of sales—the revenue it generates. Sales success comes from focusing on the activities that lead to the revenue we want. The only way to determine the activities that work is to discover and document your successful sales process.

People sell to people. Only by active listening and coaching can you help your sales people achieve higher performance. Use these challenges to help you focus on the sales activities and conversations that will generate revenue:

1. If you don't have a formal sales process, lead a project in the next month to extract the best practices from your top sales people. Use this to create and implement a sales process in the next 90 days.

2. Create measurable sales activities that must be completed in order to move an individual deal ahead and measure these activities over time.

3. In the next week, listen to at least five sales calls with your sales manager, providing feedback to the sales person and your sales manager.

PRODUCT STRATEGY

It was February 2011. Karalee and I had decided to purchase a new sailboat, leave Canada, and home school our children for two years while living on the sailboat in the Mediterranean. The question was "What boat?"

Over the previous twenty years we had owned three boats, so we had a pretty good idea of what did and didn't work for us. In the end it came down to five critical factors: comfort (big enough for five people to live on), performance (needed to sail easily and well), availability (we wanted to be sailing in the summer), price (we had a budget number we planned to stick to), and finally storage. We decided on a Jeanneau 43DS which we named Dragonsinger. It met our budget, more than six large drawers were filled with books and materials that would be needed to teach Jocelyn, Kevin, and Allen a year of school, there was room for each of us, and it was a joy to sail.

Jeanneau are adept at reading the mass market for sailboats. They continuously design and introduce new models. They use best-of-breed manufacturing methods to keep production high and costs low. This lets Jeanneau deliver beautiful and high quality products to the market at a price that makes their competitors envious. Dragonsinger never let us down, a testament to the quality of the design and build of the Jeanneau 43DS.

START SMALL AND FAST

In the mid-80s, Bob Green and I were going full blast building Robelle. When we were not travelling and giving presentations at trade shows, user group meetings, and at other events, we were back home with our heads down writing software. We found that the telephone could be incredibly detrimental to our creativity and productivity. Calling each other to book lunch together the following week was an interruption. Interrupting each other to brainstorm a solution to a tough technical problem was perfectly acceptable. The problem was that the telephone didn't distinguish between these two events.

Bob and I liked the idea of snail mail. We could get the mail when we wanted. Communication on the telephone happened when the caller wanted, not when we wanted. Our only problem with snail mail was that it was too slow.

Bob and I sat down and designed the key components of an electronic mail package. An In Box, Out Box, and a Filing Cabinet. I had a weekend free and late on a Friday afternoon I sat down on the keyboard and started to code Xpress, the electronic mail package we would end up developing and selling to over 200 customers world-wide. I worked throughout the weekend and by leveraging the best-of-breed development practices we had created, I was able to release the first version of Xpress on Monday. Bob, Annabelle, and I used the first version. We immediately found a few issues, which I quickly fixed. We continued to develop Xpress internally and within a year had released it as a complete product to the HP 3000 marketplace. Some of the key takeaways from this experience still hold true today:

1. Be clear on whom you are building the product for and what pains you are solving.

2. Put a working version into the hands of users as soon as possible.

3. Constantly iterate in short cycles (two weeks for software).

4. Use the product yourself.

FOCUS ON THE PAIN

If you ask most people what their problem is, they will tell you a symptom. The truth is that most people don't really know what they need, let alone want. To identify a true need, ask the question why three times. When someone first tells you what their problem is, respond with "tell me why that is such a problem for you?" By the time you have asked why three times you will either be close to the real pain points or the person you are talking with is the wrong one.

People pay to solve big headaches. As has been succinctly said to me:

> Discover the pain points by asking the question why three times.

"The bigger the headache and the stronger your pain pill, the higher the price and faster the sale."

Many times in my career I have attempted to create solutions that satisfied a need, only to learn that no one would pay me to satisfy that need. Clearly there are exceptions—if you are hungry enough, you will eat at pretty much any restaurant. But given a choice of restaurants, your need for cleanliness and nutritional food will have a big impact on where you eat.

WHOLE PRODUCT

All too often I have heard myself and others claim that "it works in the lab." A working prototype is not a product. Products are surrounded by many things that make it possible for people to experience, purchase, deliver, install, and use the product successfully. You can purchase a gas stove from a retailer, but someone has to deliver the stove, get the gas correctly hooked up to it, have the gas connection inspected, and then you need to learn how to use the stove. Everyone involved in your experience is far removed from the factory where the stove was made.

Many engineers focus on features and benefits. Product managers and entrepreneurs need to focus on the entire customer experience. Does the customer need to try the product first before they will buy? If so, does your product, staff, and systems support a try before you buy process?

USER TOUCH POINTS

In the Harvard Business Review post For a Breakthrough Idea, Start by Examining Customer Touch Points[4], Brian Klapper describes how a retail bank reduced its call volume by new users who set up a line of credit by 40%. They achieved this by focusing on every touch point new customers had in setting up their line of credit. The team then redesigned every single touch point to create a completely different customer experience. Not only did the customer experience dramatically change, they now understood the line of credit product, how to use it, and how dipping into their line of credit would show up in their banking statements.

Just as we must have a clear notion of everyone involved in the buying process for our product, we need to clearly model all the users of our products and services, not only the direct users who interact with the product, but also all those who derive value from the product indirectly. An accounting solution will have many people in the accounting department who use the product. The reports that the accounting solution produces may be of far greater value than the activities of the accounting department. A whole product view that sees the entire value chain of everyone that is touched by the product ensures that you are fully solving the pain you set out to solve. It also ensures that you can extract the maximum value possible from your product.

TRY BEFORE YOU BUY

The Robelle model let people try out our software products for one month before purchasing them. We built software and systems to:

1. Be capable of creating tapes with a custom version of the software with the customer's company name and an embedded expiry date.

2. Designed and built a special program that could change the

---

4   blogs.hbr.org/2013/11/for-a-breakthrough-idea-start-by-examining-customer-touch-points/

expiry date at a customer site using special codes that were very difficult to hack.

3. Made our customer relationship management system remind sales people when a trial was about to expire.

4. Modified our products to inform customers when their trial was about to expire.

It is tempting to skip over all of this work. We closed many sales at Robelle because:

1. The prospects could implement the software in their own environment, and

2. We closed the sale within a day once the software expired, because our software solved a very difficult pain point for these prospects that they had come to rely on during the one-month trial period.

ECOSYSTEM

It is rare that a sophisticated product can be fully made, shipped, sold, installed, trained for, and used by the people at just your company. Building a trusted ecosystem lets you build a whole product and provides

> You create a whole product by building an **ECOSYSTEM** to support all aspects of buying delivering, and supporting your product or service.

a completely satisfying customer experience. Even something as simple as toothpaste needs to go through a long supply chain before you can purchase it at your favorite grocery or drug store.

Not all partners are created equal. As you build your whole product and support system, create processes for finding, validating, training, and monitoring your partners. At Robelle, we hosted a meeting at one of our international distributor sites where all our distributors were invited. We used the two-day meeting for new product announcements, road map discussions, tricky customer problem reviews, and for open discussions with our distributors and our own business. We were the only North

American partner that did this with the international distributors (who often represented several different vendors). It was a lot of effort, but in the end we built better products, better systems, had better distributors, happier customers, and made more money than our competitors.

MINIMUM VIABLE PRODUCT

Earlier, I described how I was able to write an electronic mail system in a weekend that could be used by three people. Not long after, we shipped early versions of the product to some interested customers.

Today we would call this the minimum viable product. The keys to an MVP are:

1. Develop it fast and get real customer feedback.
2. Force yourself to test all aspects of your infrastructure with the MVP: demoing, purchasing, delivering, and supporting.
3. Iterate fast and often.
4. Solve a big pain point for a recognized group of people who all share the same pain.
5. Use the initial feedback to build the model of who your ideal first customers will be.

Some product lines, software for example, make this much easier than other types of products. You can get feedback and even start selling without having the physical product completed.

PACKAGING

Apple is one of the leaders in the technology field in combining incredible form into a compelling package. From the visual delight of seeing an iPhone or iPad to the feeling of holding one in your hands, there is a positive visceral response to these devices.

In today's age of instant communication, tweets, and email, I think many of us have lost sight of ways we can surprise and delight our prospects and customers with physical forms. There are many ways you can think about physical forms as you interact with your customers. Here are a few:

1. Send a personal handwritten note to prospects and customers, and with products when they are shipped. Purdys[5], a successful Chocolatier, includes the name of the person who inspected the chocolates in every box of chocolates they ship. A personal note differentiates you from almost everyone else out there.

2. If prospects, customers, or employee recruits visit your office, think through their experience from the time they first enter the door until the time they leave. What are the first things they see? What do they feel if they sit down to wait? Once they get past reception, what impression do they get of the people and the physical three-dimensional experience of your premises?

3. If you send a physical product, consider the entire packaging. What will the customer experience be when they receive your product and first open it up?

Physical form does matter. Think through the packaging of all of your products and customer interactions. Use those interactions to improve the brand experience and impression that everyone has of your company.

PRODUCT LAUNCHES

Launching a new product is an exhilarating process. While fast moving and dynamic, product launches have many of the same key elements.

Ready: When is the new product ready to be launched? In engineering driven organizations, some will think it is ready when it works in the lab. In operationally oriented organizations it may be when every single aspect of delivering and supporting the product is ready. In marketing driven organizations, it may be ready when you can demonstrate it to a customer in a PowerPoint presentation. You need to define what ready means.

Whole Product: Successful product launches focus on the whole product experience for the prospect and customer. Even if only a portion of the whole product experience will be available at first launch, map out the full experience and decide what you can and cannot live with in the first release.

> Successful product launches need everyone to be involved in both the planning and the implementation of all phases of the launch.

Involve Everyone: Marketing will need weeks to months to even a year of advance notice to fully develop all the materials needed to successfully support the communications and marketing of a new product. This includes high quality product screen shots or photographs that will be needed. Including customer support, manufacturing, sales teams, and IT, essentially every department has to be involved for a successful product launch.

Communication and Channels: To maximize early sales of your new product, you must start your communications in advance of the product launch. Build up demand through your entire sales channel by creating anticipation for the product. This is where coordination is critical. Follow through on all of your deadlines to keep momentum and to ensure that you deliver on your promises.

Training: New products require a lot of training of your internal staff, sales channels, support people, and everyone involved in your ecosystem to create a whole product experience for customers. Budget and plan for training, in time and money.

Feedback: Gather feedback from all key stakeholders all through the launch process. This includes internal and external resources, partners, suppliers, and everyone else with a stake in the success of the product launch. It will never be perfect at first release, so build in a second release as part of the product build and launch plan.

Keep it up: You create a new product, launch it, and then forget about it. A sustained marketing, communications, and subsequent release plan keeps interest and sales moving forward. Once you get your first referential quotes from happy customers, start broadcasting and using those to further enhance the reputation of your new product.

AHEAD, BEHIND, OR IN THE MIDDLE

Products are always in some sort of flux. In your markets, you are either ahead, behind, or in the middle of the product curve. Know where you sit in the product life cycle and make strategic decisions about where you want to be in the future with each of your products. All products have a start, middle, and end. You need a product life cycle strategy, rather than believing that your products will last forever.

What sales person has lamented being asked yet again "What's new with you and your company?" Products evolve over time. Treat each new evolution of your product as an opportunity for a new product launch. Not all changes will justify every step in your full-blown product launch check list, but having the check list allows you to make the decision about what to include in releasing new versions of your product.

ONE HUNDRED CONVERSATIONS

There is a rule of thumb in product management that you have to have at least one hundred conversations with people to deeply understand what is needed in a product. It takes that many conversations to gain clarity about what is driving people to consider a product, what their pain points are, and what are the top two or three pains they would really like to solve by purchasing and using a product.

> Assume you know nothing until you have had 100 conversations with prospects and customers.

In the formative phase of a company, the founder often has these conversations. Or the founder comes from a background where they have enough history and conversations in an industry to have had one hundred conversations. You need to make sure that as you continue to grow your company that those coming behind you in product management have the same opportunities to have these conversations and gain their own sense of the market, people, pain, and solutions.

REPEATABILITY

Successful products are built on top of successful processes. There are many ways that a customer experiences a product. All of those experiences must be supported over time. Your product strategy needs to include all of these touch points in the design.

Think through all the major organizational areas that you need to think through to reliably and repeatedly be capable of delivering the same customer experience over and over again. We touch on many of these areas in other chapters, but give you this list so that the information is gathered in one place from a product point of view. It is easy to forget about one or more of them when you are creating and releasing outstanding products.

> **R&D:** What do your development processes look like? How do you keep engineers in conversation with selected users? What's your process for choosing product features and managing initial and subsequent versions of the product?

> **Manufacturing:** How to you build your product? Is your supply chain fully integrated and visible in the manufacturing process? Are all dependencies and timelines identified?

> **Fulfillment:** How do you make sure that what the customer ordered is what the customer actually receives? What are your delivery timelines and how do you meet them?

> **Sales:** What is the process involved in buying your product? How does your product support this? How is quoting done?

Support: Who answers questions about your product before, during, and after the sales cycle? How are returns handled? What about warrantee and repairs? How can you engineer support calls out of the product?

Enhancements: How do you plan, build, and release future versions of the product? How is everyone on this list kept informed and trained as new versions of the product are brought to market?

Product strategy is as much about processes as about vision. Define those processes in all aspects of the product life cycle to maximize the revenue and value you receive from your product investment.

Case Study:
MURRAY GOLDBERG, FOUNDER MARINE LEARNING SYSTEMS

Serial entrepreneur Murray Goldberg created one of the world's first online learning management systems (LMS) for universities and corporations. After seeing exponential growth, Murray exited the company he created, only to discover an entirely new industry with unique needs for training and learning management systems. Murray is using his product management and software expertise to solve a global problem that affects anyone who travels the world's oceans.

BACKGROUND

BC Ferries provides critical transportation services to the west coast of Canada. It runs one of the largest ferry systems in the world, providing services for passengers and vehicles to 47 terminals along 24 routes with a fleet of 35 vessels. BC Ferries carries approximately 19 million passengers and 7 million vehicles each year.

BC Ferries' core value is first and foremost safety. In 2006, a critical safety event led BC Ferries to commit to strive to "have the best training in the world."

Murray was engaged by BC Ferries as a member of a team tasked with designing a state of the art training program. While Murray had no maritime expertise, BC Ferries understood that technology was a critical tool in any modern, effective training program, and hoped Murray could contribute his expertise in learning technologies.

VESSEL SPECIFIC LEARNING

Murray worked as a member of a team attempting to devise a short training program. There was no technology involved. Ten people went through the pilot program and in Murray's words "It worked out really, really well." The experience was very positive both in terms of trainee experience and training outcomes. With this success, BC Ferries decided to roll the program out to the entire base of operational employees– roughly 4,000 people.

The group identified the key requirements of an effective commercial maritime electronic training program:

- Capable of training for core competencies (non-vessel specific)
- Specific training unique to each vessel and the particular mix of equipment used on that vessel
- Systems must work onboard ships far away from any Internet connections
- They must also work equally well in a home environment away from the ship

It was clear that to scale the pilot program, technology would be needed. While there were LMSes that could handle core competencies, there were none that could be configured on a per-vessel basis. There were also none that worked equally well when connected to the Internet as when on a vessel with no or limited Internet access. After Murray found that there was no LMS capable of dealing with BC Ferries' requirements he created MarineLMS. Using his eLearning expertise he embarked on what turned out to be a multi-year process of product development and refinement.

VESSEL KNOWLEDGE

Understanding your role within the context of a specific vessel is a key part of training and marine safety. The moment a crew member steps on a ship they have to understand the equipment on that vessel, the layout of the vessel, and the routines for that vessel, a process known in the industry as familiarization. It's a lot of learning that is very specific to, not your job itself, but where you are doing your job.

There was no efficient mechanism to do this while achieving standardized, effective and measurable training outcomes. The way it's done normally is through a process of job shadowing in which a new employee follows a more experienced employee for a period of time to learn from them. This introduces a lot of variability in training outcomes – outcomes which are highly dependent on the knowledge of the person being shadowed and his or her ability to train. In the end, there is no way to standardize this form of training. There is no way to measure it and therefore no way to manage it. Before the new BC Ferries program, this was the way the majority of commercial marine training took place.

UNIQUE PRODUCT CAPABILITIES

What Marine Learning Systems did was build a new LMS (MarineLMS) that dynamically created learning resources for the vessel-specific training automatically. It also uses an adaptive learning approach. Inside the LMS is a database where each piece of equipment, its learning materials, and the relationships between the different types of vessel equipment and routines for using them are documented. For example, if you are a deckhand trainee, you go on to the system and say "I need to be trained to be a deckhand" and the LMS will ask "For which vessel and on what routes?" The deckhand then selects those and the system reaches into a database, selecting the learning for all those items that are specific to that vessel and its routes to create a seamless, cohesive package. The end result is essentially an online textbook, customized to that particular trainee, in the chosen position, working on the indicated vessel and route. It is a customized learning resource that looks as though it was built by hand for the unique needs of each trainee.

The magic in the software is that there could be 900 different versions of a particular scenario. No one could ever build the training by hand and maintain it. Since the technology does it automatically, it is easy, making it a powerful tool for a maritime organization. If there is one particular model of radar on 10 of their 40 ships they document it once in the learning database and put the tags in the database, indicating that these ten ships have this particular radar. When an employee sits down to learn for 'shipX', it brings in the right radar unit, the right ECIDS machine, the right routines, the right anchor and emergency equipment, and so on. There is nothing in the industry except for MarineLMS that can do this.

EXPANDING BEYOND BC FERRIES

In the first four years of use at BC Ferries, MarineLMS has been hugely successful. It's part of their SailSafe program, a larger culture safety transformation program at BC Ferries in partnership with the BC Ferry & Marine Workers' Union. There is more to it than just MarineLMS and they have done amazingly well. For example, their insurance rates have dropped by three quarters and their accent rate has dropped by 60%.

With these exceptional results, Murray stepped back and realized that BC Ferries was not the only organization facing these challenges. Murray then embarked on an ambitious project to build a brand new version that could be used by any commercial maritime organization to train their employees. While only three quarters of the way through creating the new MarineLMS, people in the industry started hearing about what Murray and his team were creating.

The need was so great in the industry that Marine Learning Systems started acquiring customers for the new MarineLMS product with no marketing and no sales team. Many of these customers are global brands with household name recognition, including cruise lines, maritime training centers, ferry operators and shipping companies. Murray still wants to fulfill his overall product architecture, but he is using these early customer successes to validate the product and guide future product development and prioritization.

CREATING CHANGE

It hasn't been easy. The maritime industry is a very traditional industry where old tried and true traditions can come into conflict with new, proven technologies. This is a challenge because MarineLMS requires a certain degree of disruptive culture change. On the positive side, there are many in the industry (both young, new executives and more mature forward thinkers) who are pushing the industry into the 21st century.

Commercial maritime operators invest heavily in their training and systems. Murray and his team have proved that MarineLMS is a more effective way to train people, creating higher levels of knowledge and safety in the industry. In addition to creating cultural changes, there are many practical challenges to getting an organization to change their training system. Murray has been open to developing custom add-ons to the core architecture of MarineLMS to fit the operational context for specific customers. In this way, existing customers define the development path of MarineLMS.

This same technology applies to any multi-sited, complex, industrial training context (resource, transportation, manufacturing, plant operations). Marine Learning Systems are planning to expand their focus. While still retaining a very solid maritime foundation, they are expanding the team to scale the company and product both in maritime and new industries.

LESSONS LEARNED

Marine Learning Systems is Murray's third company. He brings a wealth of product knowledge, software engineering expertise, and entrepreneurship to a global problem. What we can learn from this experience is that it is helpful to:

1. Identify a critical problem that an organization must solve.
2. Use a pilot project to identify the key aspects of the problem and what is needed as a potential solution.
3. Keep in mind when building a custom solution for a customer that you might one day productize it.
4. Have an architectural vision and let early commercial success help guide what must be done first.

5. Use cash flow from custom solutions to help build your business while staying true to the overall architectural vision you have for the product.

When travelling by sea, we take our safety for granted. The truth is that we are only as safe as the quality of the training of those who are operating the vessel we are on. Marine Learning Systems and Murray Goldberg are making marine travel safer for all of us.

TAKE ACTION NOW

Until you have a product or service, you have nothing to sell. Even small changes in your thinking about your product strategy can have impactful results. How you demonstrate, sell, and deliver your product have an enormous impact on your sales cycle. Customers want a product that is surrounded by everything they need to use it successfully. We call this a whole product. Customers are one of the best sources of feedback on how easy it is to receive and use your product. Follow these suggestions to dramatically improve your products before this quarter finishes:

1. Identify one product change that your team can implement in the next 30 days that would speed up the sales process and implement and release that change in the subsequent 60 days.

2. Review one of your products this quarter from the "whole product" view and document what is missing to make it perfect for your ideal customer. Share the document with all key stakeholders in your ecosystem and ask them for their feedback.

3. Call three new customers in the next week and interview them about their experience of receiving, setting up, and using your product or service.

PEOPLE STRATEGY

While travelling in the Mediterranean, we were staying in Barcelona where we watched a group of visiting youths from the Balearic Islands create a human castle, called a castell. Our family had been watching these groups prepare, dance, and then gather together to build competing castells. Even though we could not understand their language, there was a strong sense of community among the groups. They had a shared culture, history, and goal, qualities we want in our businesses.

Gwyn Teatro writes in *Guiding Rookies ~ Three Steps To Doing It Well*[6] of her experience in bringing new employees into an organization. Her first guideline is to "Help Them Connect to..."

- Organizational purpose
- Values on which the organization is built
- Internal and external networks

In short, connect to the broad community the organization represents. By connecting and being part of a community with a shared vision and goals, we can create great things. The youths building the castells in Barcelona had a clear organization purpose, shared values and a history to build upon, and we watched their internal and external networks at work as they competed against teams from different areas. To maximize business performance, this is the experience you should create for every employee in your business.

6   gwynteatro.wordpress.com/2011/05/15/guiding-rookies-three-steps-to-doing-it-well/

CHANGE THE ENVIRONMENT

In life if we change the environment, we change our experience. All too often, I see people being boxed into their cubicles; creative people who don't have access to spontaneous workspaces and white boards and software engineers who are supposed to invent things by staring at their screens.

I know that time and time again my best ideas have come from getting out of the office, going for a walk and connecting with the beauty of British Columbia.

For executives, this is as important. How can you achieve breakthroughs in strategy if your quarterly meeting takes place in an office boardroom? To truly change and grow a business, you need to get away from the day-to-day fires, turn off the phones, and meet in a neutral environment far removed from the office. You then have a chance to foster new ways of connecting, fresh ideas for strategy, and renewed energy to push off in new directions.

Building work environments that are flexible, encouraging teams to collaborate somewhere outside the office, and letting people customize and change their environment creates outstanding experiences and performance.

CHALLENGE PEOPLE TO BLOOM

As a leader at Robelle I often gave people tasks that challenged them to raise their own performance and leadership. Kerry Lathwell, who reported to me for ten years, shared with me after our time together that time and time again I asked her to do things that she knew inside herself she could not do. And every time she was able to do it.

Like watching a beautiful plant grow and blossom into a beautiful flower, how do you help people in your organization blossom and raise their own and others' potential? Try these ideas:

Have belief. There was never a time that I asked Kerry to do something that I didn't believe that she was not capable of.

Make sure one person is accountable. In team efforts, there still needs to be one person that is accountable for the team, even if that person does not have control of all the individuals and resources on the team that are needed for the task.

Set measurable goals. Simply wanting more customers isn't a goal. Wanting ten new customers by December 31st of this year is a goal.

Let people fail safely. You might not want to risk the entire future of the business to a junior employee with great potential. You do want to give that person a task that challenges them and that, should they fail, the organization can still recover from.

Cultivate a culture that encourages people to stretch themselves. Not only does this encourage people to increase their own performance, but their example spurs others to push beyond their own limits.

ATTRACTION

If you want to attract talented individuals to your business, you need to stand out from the crowd. All of the marketing and communication that you do for your customers will also form part of what attracts people to your company. When you look at your web site, social media platforms, and press coverage, be sure to look for these things:

Current: Make your company looks modern and appealing. Attracting young people today requires Twitter feeds and blog postings if those people are going to take your company seriously.

> Attracting the right people to your business is a marketing challenge. Appeal to those that share your core values.

Collaboration: Act in a collaborative way so that you attract people who want to collaborate. People today are looking for a way to make a difference by combining their efforts with other people.

Challenges: Talented individuals thrive on challenges. When doing career outreach, show career paths and ways to solve problems that can help individuals reach their next level of performance.

Top performers like to work with other top performers. If you want to be a highly effective organization, you need to attract highly skilled and motivated individuals. Use powerful communication and collaboration activities to attract the high performing individuals you want.

COMMUNICATION

My son Allen and I sometimes go treasure hunting by Geocaching[7]. Geocachers leave hidden caches (there is almost certainly one near you) and then publish the latitude and longitude of the cache, along with hints on how to find it. If you have never geocached, you might think that knowing the latitude and longitude would guarantee that you could find the cache. This is rarely the case.

GPS units, used to locate your latitude and longitude, and the GPS system itself, are only accurate to a few meters (or yards if that's how you measure things). Geocachers are experts at hiding their caches. You can be within an arm's reach of the cache and still not be able to find it without the help of the hints given with each geocache.

Like geocaches, strategic plans are supposed to make it clear where an organization is aiming for. Consider these ideas on how you communicate your strategic plans:

1. Good strategic plans have a clear destination.
2. While the destination might be clear to senior management, the destination is often lost in terms of how it is communicated. If you were told to meet outside "10 Downing Street" you would be more likely to arrive at Whitehall in London, England than if you were given latitude 51.5N, and longitude 0.1W. Humans work better with human references.

....

7   geocaching.com

3. Even if we have the destination in both human terms and in latitude and longitude, we can be helped to find our destination with hints. Saying we will meet on the street closest to the home of the British Prime Minister gives us a lot more context to work with. Many strategic plans do not provide the context everyone needs to find the destination.

4. If you are meeting at "10 Downing Street" and you are coming from Vancouver, Canada you might need a lot more guidance than if you are coming from Birmingham, England. Most strategic plans are missing the intermediate guideposts that help each individual make their way to the destination.

In addition to communicating your strategic plan clearly, you also need to regularly communicate how you are doing against your strategic plan in a way that each of your employees can relate to. Just

> Employees need to hear regular and clear communication on your strategic plan and progress.

like your strategic goals should be explained in different ways so that different people can understand them, you need to do the same when communicating your progress. The key is to have regular communication and then get feedback on whether everyone is getting what you are communicating.

INVESTING IN YOUR TALENT

When we launched Dragonsinger, the sailboat we lived on for two years, it came with a full set of modern instruments. There were a lot of them. In addition to speed, log, and wind instruments, Dragonsinger included an integrated chart plotter and radar display. It came as a complete surprise to me how challenging it was to discover how to use all these instruments. At the time I had twenty years boating experience. I have a degree in computer science. I love technical devices. And still I struggled.

While my children were home schooling themselves, I was reading through the instrument manuals. At the dock, I would turn the instruments on and play with them. When we finally got Dragonsinger moving, I turned the instruments on and really understand how much I still had to learn. After I climbed the learning curve, I then had to teach Karalee, Jocelyn, Kevin, and Allen how to use the instruments.

There were several things I learned from this experience:

1. Even when you have a lot of experience and training, there can still be a big learning curve.

2. Stay motivated to keep learning. For me, having the safety of my family at stake kept me motivated to keep learning.

3. Hands on learning is far more effective than book learning or "learning at the dock".

4. The best learning comes from interaction. I learned the most about Dragonsinger's instruments from other cruisers and from my children.

In a business context, we need to keep these lessons in mind. To help them be the best they can be, we have to invest in our employee's initial and ongoing training. Do so within the context of your business so that they can learn what applies to your business. Invest at least a week's worth of training for every person in your organization every year. It is a solid employee retention strategy and a proven way to help your people be more productive. They will deeply appreciate the investment you make in them.

I have educated through articles, white papers, webinars, blogs, presentations, and on-site sessions. Even with this experience, it is easy for me to forget what it is like to be at the bottom of the learning curve, struggling to make my way forward. When I'm forgetful, I remember the Dragonsinger experience and remind myself of how hard it was to learn our instruments and climb the learning curve, even when I was doing what I love. Help everyone in your organization climb their own learning curves. To grow and improve, never stop your or their learning.

COLLABORATION

To accelerate your organization's performance, learn how to help people collaborate. We build silos within our departments. To succeed today, you need to get a wide variety of people from all departments to work together.

Thinking about collaboration in terms of music and how an orchestra works together can be a powerful metaphor to coordinate your individuals and teams.

> **Time.** Music is broken into time signatures and bars. Each bar has a given number of beats. The tempo sets the overall time for how fast the beats go. When we coordinate people, our meetings, deliverables, and other rhythms set the beat. As leaders we set the tempo for how fast we want the organization to go.
>
> **Individuals.** Each line in sheet music represents a different instrument or voice. These individual lines are combined to create the overall sound we hear. In organizations, we need to provide clarity to individuals as to what is expected of them. It is rare to provide the level of clarity that is provided by each line and note of music.
>
> **Movement.** Each line of music can be going in different directions, each note can have different lengths, and the emphasis we put on individual notes can vary moment by moment. This level of precision is rarely seen in organizations, yet is often needed to deliver on complex projects.
>
> **Orchestration.** When you listen to the individual parts of a score of a large group or orchestra, each can sound completely different than the finished score. A beautifully written piece of music comes together as each individual part is combined to form something greater than the sum of all the parts. When we get teams to perform at that level, we achieve the same thing for our organizations.

Higher performing teams know how to orchestrate themselves to bring out the best in each individual, while ensuring that the complete picture is delivered in a beautifully coordinated way for customers.

USE ADVERSITY TO BUILD TEAMS

Great performing organizations learn how to set a vision and then motivate all leaders and employees to collaborate together to pursue that vision. For many organizations, building trust between leaders, between employees, and between each other is critical to becoming a high performing organization.

When challenges arise in your business, use the adversity to get your teams to collaborate and work together to solve what has come up. See who takes their game up a notch to overcome the challenge. These are often early signs of your next leaders. Where you can do so safely, put individuals and teams in situations where they have to overcome barriers. Let people build trust in each other and their ability to work together.

LISTEN FOR THE LAUGHTER

Whenever I work with teams, I listen for the laughter. If I pass a meeting dealing with a tough issue and I can hear a few laughs from time-to-time, I know that everyone is on track. I know that all too often, I take things too seriously (see Leaders Set the Tone). There is a lot of power in being able to laugh at ourselves and see the humor in a situation.

HUMOR and laughter can bring teams together.

There is a big difference between laughing at someone and laughing with someone. Building strong and trusting relationships means not taking personal shots at people. It is the art of showing our own and others' foibles in a gentle and respectful light. You can keep peer pressure up for team goals. If you need to coach around personal performance, do so in private. Even there, you can put people at ease by sharing a humorous anecdote about when you were less than perfect to start the conversation.

COOK TOGETHER

For almost two decades at Robelle, we supplied the food and everyone supplied the effort to make lunch every day. This started because we had an office on a farm in Langley, a rural community outside of Vancouver where the office was originally a separate apartment at the end of the house. This included a kitchen.

When Robelle was small, cooking lunches every day started and continued when we moved into a "real" office thirteen years after the company was started. The office included a full kitchen, fridge, table, and chairs where we would eat together every day.

Making and eating lunch together connects us outside of the work context. This creates healthy relationships with each other as people. Building those person-to-person relationships is what lets you build trust together as a team.

CREATIVE PEOPLE

Innovative businesses and products are created by people. One summer day my friend, Becky Robinson, CEO of Weaving Influence, reminded me of the simplicity of inspiring children to be creative:

"My girls haven't colored much this summer. Yesterday, I bought a new box of crayons. They've been coloring nonstop. If I had known that was all it would take, I would have bought them a new box of crayons sooner."

Becky's comment reminded me of our three children, coloring, exploring, and drawing. When I read Becky's comments, I could even smell the box of crayons. What wonderful creations my children created when we gave them space, time, and tools. When dealing with adults and organizations, we seem to lose sight of these simple ideas.

> **Space.** Give your people enough space to color, explore, and create. Are there enough communal tables? Enough white boards?

Enough screens to connect laptops to? Enough chances to collaborate together?

Time. Is everyone's schedule so tightly booked with meetings and interactions that they never have time to think through issues, innovate, and be creative?

Tools. Are we stingy with the tools we give people thinking that it is more important to save money that to build environments that create innovation and new ideas? Many tools cost little more than crayons and paper.

Everyone has creative potential. You create the environment that can help or hinder that creativity.

HANDLING EMAIL

Back around 1985, Bob Green and I were probably two of a few hundred people who came up with the idea of host-based electronic email. At that time, many businesses had computers that employees were logging onto every day and those computers were becoming powerful enough to host email applications.

Bob's and my original vision was simple. We were building Robelle into a successful software company. Bob and I needed lengthy periods to design and program our solutions. The telephone interrupted us,

> Set email expectations appropriately to remove the burden of email from you and your employees.

disrupting the intense focus we needed to build world-class products. We liked regular mail (snail mail is what we call it today), because we got to choose when we got the mail from the mailbox. The only problem was that it was too slow for our communication needs; thus was born the idea for an electronic version of our real mailbox. Bob and I could send messages and the receiver could choose when to read the messages.

Fast forward thirty years. I feel like Bob's and my original vision of email as a communication medium where the receiver could choose when to get messages has been lost on a generation of smartphone users. People walk down the street, completely ignoring what is going on around them, answering email like Bob and I used to answer the telephone. Over time the expectation of instant response to email has crept into society.

We pay a price for how we treat email. People cannot always be tuned in and turned on. It is critical that clear and accountable expectations be set around email policies and responsiveness. I believe that for people to be effective they must have time off away from the business. The policy I hold to is that I never respond to work emails outside of normal business hours. If it is both important and urgent, anyone is free to text or call my cell phone.

It takes discipline to set, communicate, and hold yourself and everyone else to these policies. For example, when I am travelling, especially for events that happen on weekends, I can easily start sending emails asking for things. Just because I am travelling or working on a weekend, does not mean I have the right to set that expectation for those that work around or for me.

In his book Expel the Elephants[8] Kevin Lawrence provides concrete steps you can take to use email to boost performance, not hinder it. Kevin reminds us of this truth about email:

"I have yet to see a job description that says 'must have high competency in responding to email.' People are not hired to respond to email, yet their lives become burdened by their inbox."

Case Study:
BART COPELAND, CEO ACTIVESTATE

What do you do when you have helped build a successful software company, attracted some of the best technical talent in the world, and are achieving steady double-digit top-line revenue growth? Bart Copeland,

8   coachkevin.com/wp-content/uploads/2010/04/elephant_final.pdf

CEO, the Management Team, and the board of directors of ActiveState faced this challenge. What they did might surprise you.

BACKGROUND

The roots of ActiveState go back to the late 2000s, when popular programming languages like Perl and Python were being developed (these are used extensively in web sites, IT applications, and other mission-critical IT infrastructure). While the tools themselves were free, they were not supported. Like many open source projects, ActiveState provided support for these languages for commercial customers who value stable and reliable environments and solutions. Remarkably, 97% of the Fortune 1000 use ActiveState's pre-compiled binary distributions of Perl, Python, or Tcl.

ActiveState also developed Komodo, a multi-language integrated development environment that dramatically improves the productivity of programmers using these and other programming languages. ActiveState attracted some of the best technical talent in the world in these areas where today Komodo is the leading development tool.

Combined together, both the language binary distributions and Komodo are used by over two million developers around the world today.

WHY CHANGE?

For many management teams an industry-leading solution with consistent year-over-year revenue growth would be enough; however, in mid-2010, the management team took a hard look at their business. The team wanted to look for opportunities that could drive triple-digit growth. Why? The leading technology companies that were truly pushing the boundaries of greatness were growing in the triple digits (at least the new product lines were). ActiveState's management team wanted ActiveState to be one of those companies. They also felt it would mean that ActiveState's employees could grow in their respective roles, as employee growth is very important to management. They also realized that they could sustain their growth but there was going to come a time, they didn't know when, that things would start leveling off. When that happened, the market would not see the value in what ActiveState has to offer.

People and innovation were the heart of the ActiveState organization. They had been missing aggressive innovation and new product offerings that leveraged their existing technology, core competencies, technical expertise, and what they had as an organization. The goal was nothing short of setting up ActiveState for hyper growth and the next phase of ActiveState's evolution.

PEOPLE FIRST

For all the Activators (how ActiveState employees are known inside and outside the company), the status quo would not be an engaging, motivating environment—they wouldn't be pushing the envelope. The fear was that ActiveState would start losing employees to newer, more exciting opportunities in the ever-changing development world of the Internet. While there was no short-term pain point in the company, this was the key long-term challenge the management team felt they faced.

What they did next was to have trust in the Activators to define what the future of ActiveState should look like. They empowered the whole company to be involved in this. Whether it was an individual working at a workstation or even the CEO, they decided, "Let's let the company run with this." Wanting to create innovation, the management team deliberately set up a period of personal innovation at ActiveState. They let people contribute ideas on anything in a series of phases.

IDEAS TO PLAN

In the first phase anyone could suggest an idea. There was a lot of visibility because they had an email list where all of the ideas and discussions were made visible for all the Activators who cared and wanted to participate in the process. By suggesting the idea you had to find a certain number of Activators with different skill sets that wanted to get behind the idea. For example, you needed both someone from a product business perspective and someone from a technical perspective to buy into the idea. The process was designed to draw out the passion of the people who were behind a specific idea.

With those individuals identified, they needed to make a very quick pitch to the entire company about why they should spend more time on their idea and justify spending up to 20% of their time on taking it further. If your idea got the green light, then the initial idea group made a pitch to recruit additional people to work on the team. That group had to flush out the idea to the point that it could be pitched to an internal review team for phase two.

To make the second phase fun and impactful at the same time, they borrowed ideas from popular shows like Shark Tank and Dragon's Den. You had to present a business plan for your idea, including the technical, product, and business aspects, while being prepared to defend your idea in front of the senior management team. What made it different from those TV shows is that it was often members of the senior management team who where pitching the idea. In that case, the management "dragons" would excuse themselves from the evaluation function. Everyone knew there were conflicts of interest, but all the Activators took it in the spirit of innovation for the best interests for the future of ActiveState.

A NEW PRODUCT APPEARS

After the two idea phases, a short-list of two ideas was presented to the board and the management team recommended one of the two ideas most suitable for ActiveState and the Activators. The board agreed with management's recommendation to pursue one of the ideas with one caveat–MVP, that is, Minimal Viable Product. The spirit was to push the idea with an MVP approach, get it out in the market, learn from it, and then if the feedback was positive, go to the next iteration of MVP and repeat it as long as it still made sense. This resulted in Stackato, their new enterprise platform as a service product. Like the Komodo, Python, Perl and Tcl language binary distributions that came before, Stackato is also built on an open source platform.

We are at the start of a multi-decade transformation of the information technology industry. Applications and data have traditionally been de-ployed on infrastructure owned by the company using the applications and creating the data. With the invention of a high-speed and reliable network infrastructure, this traditional model is shifting to a cloud model where all applications and data are hosted by third-party vendors and accessed via a web browser, smart phone application, or terminal server.

A subset of cloud computing is called platform as a service (PaaS). You need to have a platform in order to deploy any application. There are many vendors of PaaS.

We are in the early days of cloud computing. There are many technical, legal, and other issues that are being worked out. Enterprises want to gain the benefits of a public PaaS, yet they are not prepared to take the risk on the security and availability of a public PaaS offering. The solution is to deploy a private platform as a service. Stackato is a platform designed specifically for enterprises to be able to easily deploy and manage platform services on their own private infrastructure, on a public infrastructure or both. Stackato and products like it are called Enterprise Private Platform as a service. It's a good thing the Activators have technical skills, because everything involved in this market is highly technical.

MARKET RESPONSE

Enterprise Private Platform is a very hot space. ActiveState estimates that the market is not even at the 20% point of being developed, yet they have received tremendous traction. ActiveState has become very strategic. All of a sudden, people all over the world are looking at ActiveState and saying, "Holy smoke, what has happened to ActiveState? They have completely transformed themselves."

ActiveState have been able to capture customers, gaining good critical mass and beating some really big players in a competitive space. The key was for the Activators to realize that they were doing this because they wanted to change the world and become much more meaningful than they had been. Although their original business was a great one, the Company wanted to play to its whole reason for being: to change people's lives with technology that just works while keeping it within the emerging cloud computing sector.

ActiveState did that with their existing products (i.e. change people's lives with technology that just works). What they are doing with Stackato is revolutionary. This can potentially impact Developers and IT workers in their day-to-day jobs. Normally taking enterprises weeks or months on the account of infrastructure, deploying an application takes only minutes with Stackato. ActiveState's customers are saying, "Why didn't I have this sooner?" That is an empowering thing for developers. Activators get excited about using technology to solve the challenges that enterprises face.

LESSONS LEARNED

When things are going well it takes true courage to step back and look at your core strategy. My take away ideas from the collaboration of Bart, his management team, and their experience at ActiveState include:

1. Never stand still.
2. Challenge yourself, the board, and your leadership team.
3. Be true to your core values.
4. Involve your employees in change.
5. Make it fun.
6. Change the world.

You know you are working with a people organization when the employees have such a fabulous name like Activators. The management team recognized that retaining their amazing team meant giving them a new challenge. By involving all the Activators in the process they are changing a trillion dollar industry.

TAKE ACTION NOW

You set the example of the values and culture for your employees. How you show up every day sets the tone for everyone in the company. The environment you work in helps you set the tone you want. High performing companies set clear goals and provide constant feedback to everyone as to how the company is doing against these goals. Email is more likely to hinder progress than it is to help, unless you set clear limits about email and you make sure you stick to your own rules. Let your people be their best, by putting the following into action:

1. In the next week, change one aspect of your environment and note the difference in how you show up and behave.

2. Communicate your goals, progress, and activities to all employees every week.

3. Set companywide limits on email and make sure that you follow them within the next 90 days.

OPERATIONAL STRATEGY

Sailing across the Atlantic Ocean in a thirty-nine foot catamaran with three other guys creates a phenomenal focus on logistics and operations. In the middle of the ocean you have to be able to look after yourself. Spare parts, provisioning, fuel, and water are just the start of the operational plans. Then, there is route planning, weather forecasting, communication, maintenance, and crew morale.

For this trip, I was principally responsible, along with the captain and owner, Dick Leighton, for all the provisioning and cooking. We had to plan for twenty-eight days—the longest Dick felt our passage could take. Plus we had Dick's 21-year-old son Andy on board. Having three children of a similar age, I knew that Andy would eat for two.

Dick and I broke it down into a weekly menu plan and from there a daily plan. As we left the Canary Islands, I monitored our daily consumption and kept track of what food was consumed. After eight days we put into the Cape Verde Islands for repairs. We were pretty accurate on our meal plans and provisioning, but I used our stop to replenish the items we were going through faster than we had planned. We would have made do, but the unplanned stop gave us a chance to adjust.

Your operational strategy may not have the lives of people at stake. You do have to come up with a plan, measure against that plan, and then make sure that you can deliver what your prospects, customers, and employees expect.

BACK OF THE ENVELOPE

My long-time accountant, Bob Cole, always told me "David, great business plans fit on the back of an envelope." Sadly, Bob is no longer with us, but his advice lives on. The key factors in your overall strategy, including your purpose, markets, business model, key financials, and cost of selling your products should fit on the back of a letter-sized envelope, or at the very least on a single sheet of paper.

> You must be able to summarize all the key aspects of your business on a single sheet of paper.

One way I gain focus on the overall business model is to "follow the money". For every dollar in revenue, write down the key activities including sales, production, collection, and profit. This is a sanity check that shows that you both understand your business model and are able to make money at what you sell.

INFORMATION TECHNOLOGY

I am biased—I have spent my entire professional career in information technology (IT). The speed of change and growth in IT makes it a necessary strategic part of every business. While IT must be strategic to your business, it does not need to be a core competency. Hiring, training, and maintaining top-level IT expertise may be better handled by a third-party.

IT must serve the needs of the business first. Since few understand the intricacies of computers, software, and how they interact, it can seem daunting to stay informed and knowledgeable. Focus on what the business needs to be successful, rather than the specifics of software and solutions. What is important is that your Customer Relationship Management (CRM) system supports your sales process, customer interactions, delivery, and product support. It is far less important that your CRM system come from a particular vendor or be the flavor of the month.

It is easy to believe that a new software application will solve all your business problems. You must focus on the business outcomes and your business processes first, and software and applications second. I have repeatedly seen improved business processes, better training, and minor improvements to existing IT systems result in enormous productivity gains for a business.

KPIS

While every business has a handful of numbers that drive their success, each business is unique in terms of which ones matter the most. Discovering what the key productivity indicators (KPIs) are for your business, how to measure them and report them, and how to improve them require a long-term focused effort.

> **HIGH PERFORMING BUSINESSES** know their top four leading indicators and top two trailing.

Every business has three to four leading indicators of success and two trailing indicators. For example, if every sale requires six conversations to close, then the number of conversations your sales people are having every day is a leading indicator of what your sales will be in the future.

Many organizations start with easy-to-measure numbers. True KPIs that predict where you are and where you are headed are rarely easy to measure, at least at first. Start with your strategy and work through your business model to discover the key activities that drive your success.

High performing organizations figure out what key numbers drive their business and create systems that report whether the business is on track. I have seen businesses that report KPIs in real-time on monitors that everyone throughout the business can see, from minute to minute. You should at least be looking at KPIs weekly while driving you and your team to monitor and respond to these numbers daily and hourly.

BENCHMARKING

It amazes me how many entrepreneurs and businesses act like they are the only ones doing what it is they do. You should have a unique brand promise that differentiates you from the rest of your competitors. While part of your business will be different, much of it will be run similarly to other businesses. Seek out the experts in each area of your business, especially if they are not in your particular industry. Network and discover what the benchmarks are for the best practices in your industry. Not only will this give you clues as to what your key productivity indicators might be, it will also give you a yardstick to see how you are performing. Deep insight often comes from outside your industry where competitive factors have driven people to find innovative and highly productive ways to get things done.

PROMISE DELIVERY SYSTEM

Marketing and advertising work best when you speak to the customer's biggest need or pain and show them how your products or services can give them what they want. In many cases, companies struggle with the effectiveness of their marketing because they talk about things that don't get the attention of their potential customers.

On the other hand, some companies are marketing masters and have a different challenge: they are not able to live up to the expectations they set to attract customers in the first place. Often, those customer ends up disappointed of feel like they were oversold or misled.

Mastery of marketing involves not only promising to fulfill the core needs and desires of your potential customers, but having the whole business built to consistently deliver on those promises—every person and process

> **PROMISE DELIVERY SYSTEM**
>
> Make a bold brand promise and then create the systems that deliver on that promise every day.

in the company from sales, to service, to reception to the back office, to the executive team and the janitorial staff.

Only through close collaboration between marketing, sales, product management, and operations can a company consistently deliver on its promise to customers. From the initial contact of a prospect, through the entire sales process, to fulfillment, and then product support, everyone in an organization must be closely aligned to deliver an outstanding customer experience. To do this over and over again requires processes, people, systems, and training along with close coordination and cooperation across departments.

These businesses that succeed at matching marketing to delivery are what we call a Promise Delivery Systems (PDS)—they make the right promises and then are fanatical about delivering on them. As a result, these PDS business can grow faster, have increased customer loyalty, and generate more referrals from existing customers.

FEEDBACK

Many in business coast along, assuming that everything is all right with their customers. You can get quite a shock if you start seeking customer feedback and realize there are a mountain of challenges your customers face with your products and services that you knew nothing about.

People often ask me how you know if your marketing messages are working. I reply that the only way to know is take your messages for a test drive and then sample your market to see what message they are receiving. Feedback often highlights large gaps in the message you think you are projecting and the message people are receiving. Here are ways you can garner customer feedback:

> **Ask for it.** At every customer interaction and after every event. Hosting a webinar? At the end, engage the participants in conversation and ask for their feedback. Finished a customer support call? Ask for feedback.

> **Survey your customers.** Do the survey online and ensure it is easy to start, pause, resume, and complete. Ask open-ended questions. While much harder to process than multiple choice questions, they provide critical insights that can help you improve your business. Remember that offering something special like a free Nano iPod (costs less than $100) to a random survey participant can improve response rates. Giveaways inject a lot of fun into the process.

Host customer events. Whether this is a customer day or a multiple day user group meeting, the key is to find ways you can provide value to your customers. While providing your value, seek feedback. Customer events produce a lot of feedback. Welcome the chance to receive it.

When you are done share your customer feedback with your customers. Open communications, admitting to your faults, and telling people what you are going to do about them builds trust. Trust builds repeat and new business.

In the end, you have to build a culture that demands customer feedback. Rather than working on the assumption that no news is good news, great companies know that constant customer feedback and improvement is the only path forward. Are you prepared to seek your customers' feedback?

CUSTOMER WOW

Garry Rasmussen built ISM-BC from a start up to $500M in revenue based on customer service excellence. He believes that no business can truly excel unless it is focused on excellence in customer service. Garry believes:

"I have not found a success story about a service where the leader was not totally committed to customer service and 'walked the talk'. When that happens the rest is magical."

Garry continues:

"As a basis for the service ethos I used a couple of books. 'Fabled Service: Ordinary Acts, Extraordinary Outcomes' by Betsy Sanders was required reading by all the management team and the story of Jan Carlson and SAS as related in the book 'At America's Service' seemed to me to epitomize the logical consequence of a true service-oriented organization."

Happy customers stick around, give you repeat business, and are easy to upsell to. Customer referrals are a powerful source of leads. Are you committed to wowing the customer?

RESPONSIVENESS

High performing companies respond fast. Response times of over sixty minutes to an inbound lead reduce your chance of being a vendor in the running. Do you even know how long it takes you to respond to an inbound lead?

If you are focused on outstanding customer service, what metrics do you use to measure both the time and quality of your responses? The same goes for returns, warranty requests, repairs, and every other touch point you have with your customers. Survey your customers about what is most important to them and their perception of your responsiveness. Then, use those results to define, measure, and report the key responsiveness measures that let your company succeed.

CUSTOMER QUALITY

Customers have told me "David, Your products are the only software I install into production without testing." In the software business, this is the ultimate compliment, but also an incredibly high standard to maintain. It took decades of hard work to build Robelle's software engineering, test, release, and feedback practices so that we could earn and keep this reputation. No matter what your business, quality as perceived by the customer is critical to your success.

EXCEPTIONS

Our business models typically focus on the common case. Generating a lead, creating a sale, building and delivering the product or service, and then collecting the revenue. Our cost structure and profitability are built on assumptions about the time and money needed to satisfy the common case.

Where we start to lose money is when there are exceptions to our business model. These exceptions can be easily ignored and often add up to enormous costs. Exceptions are friction points that hold us back. Some questions to ask yourself:

1. When are sales taking much longer than your average sales cycle?

2. What is your return policy and how is it processed?

3. How can accounts receivables be collected at a lower cost?

4. What are your average failure rates and why are they increasing?

RETURNS

High return rates indicate either poor quality or a bad customer fit. Returns cost you and the business a lot. It pays to monitor return rates and dig into why returns are happening in the first place. Reach out to customers and ask them why they are returning goods.

To help reduce return rates, focus on these areas:

1. Make your return policy clear to customers.

2. Create a "try before you buy" option.

3. Have a process for returns and document this for customers, including where and how they return the goods.

4. Ensure that at every step of the buying process the prospect understands what they are agreeing to, what they will get, and what the process is.

5. Ask for feedback when people do return items.

SUPPLIERS

Suppliers are critical to delivering your brand promise. Treat them as part of the team.

View all your suppliers as partners in delivering your business, because that is what they are—partners. Stay actively engaged with your suppliers when things are going well and you will be able to lean on those relationships if things go wrong. Have you suddenly got a massive increase in orders? Keep your suppliers in the loop so you can work together on inventory levels, deadlines, and cash flow management. You can often get special terms on orders that are strategic to your business and your suppliers.

Your promise delivery system includes your suppliers. If they don't deliver, you don't deliver. Suppliers are critical to the quality of your product, return rates, repairs, and warrantees. Choose them wisely and then put time and effort into keeping them informed on a regular basis—not just when things go sideways.

Case Study:
MIKE JAGGER, FOUNDER AND CEO PROVIDENT SECURITY

Mike Jagger is a dynamic business leader who knows how to market his services and has the key systems in place needed to consistently deliver on his brand promises. As Founder and CEO of Provident Security, Mike and his team make the promise that matters the most to their customers better than any of their competitors—to revolutionize their industry by being a Promise Delivery System.

INCREDIBLE VISION

Before Mike started Provident Security, he was amazed to learn that when an alarm goes off at a business or a residence very little happens. Most alarm companies respond with a phone call, at best. In Vancouver, Canada, where Provident Security is based, the average police response to a burglar alarm report is two hours and six minutes. Mike was convinced that customers have an expectation that when an alarm goes off, the alarm service will do something proactive. Mike saw an opportunity to deliver on customer expectations. Mike made a bold promise that speaks directly to the core concerns of his customers:

Provident promises its customers that they will be at the customer's door within five minutes of an alarm going off—guaranteed.

Mike knows what he needs to do to earn business from his customers. While many businesses stop at their customer promise, that's just where Mike starts. Mike not only communicates up front and tells the customer things to make them want to do business with him, he is almost to the point of being obsessed with delivering on that promise.

FIVE MINUTES

When Mike first founded Provident he got out a map of Vancouver and drew a circle around his headquarters which represented where he could drive to in five minutes. Unlike other alarm companies, some of which take on customers over a 5,000 square mile area, Provident focused on this one area. Mike figured that with five minutes driving time, he could satisfy his promise to be on site within five minutes of an alarm going off.

Mike and his team discovered that there is much more to getting to a residential or business customer's premises in five minutes, 24 hours a day. A single traffic light could introduce a one-minute delay into the process. Mike had a guarantee to keep and he was adamant about delivering on what he promised his customers.

Mike and his team approached the problem as a tactical military exercise and broke their five-minute response time down into 300 seconds. Second by second they looked at each part of the response they could control and the parts they couldn't. It became clear that knowing where the guards were and how to dispatch them was one of the slowest parts of the process.

In particular, the process of having an employee respond to an alarm signal on their computer screen, pick up the phone and dial the number for a mobile guard in the field was a significant time waster. As a result, Provident built customized software that automated the dispatch procedure so that when an incoming alarm is received, it is immediately and automatically relayed to the closest guard's Blackberry or iPhone within four seconds of the alarm going off. The direct message sent to the guard includes the customer's name, address, and which zone in the building or house triggered the alarm. Innovation and automation are critical factors in delivering on their five-minute promise.

KEYS, KEYS, KEYS

Getting the guards to the right place within five minutes when an alarm has gone off is only the start of the process. What is the guard supposed to do once they arrive at a residence or business where an alarm has gone off? The guard needs a key to enter the premises to see what is going on. This simple concept of the guard having access to a key at the right place and the right time is a massive challenge for Provident.

Mike and his team focused their creative energy on this challenge. It was not reasonable to have a key for every client stored in every vehicle. What if one of their vehicles was stolen? What if one of the guards was dishonest?

The solution they came up with was to have a vault box welded to every vehicle. Each vault contains six or seven key cases. Inside each key case are hundreds of manila envelopes, each one identical except for a unique number written on the outside of each envelope. If someone stole one of the vehicles, they would have thousands of keys, but no reference whatsoever to the address corresponding to each key.

When a guard has responded to an alarm and shows up on site, he makes a request to the operations center for the key number of the envelope with the key to the premises. Provident's custom system has been designed to verify that an active alarm exists at the address for which the key is being requested. Once the request has been received, someone in the operations center must authorize the request and once that's done the system issues the number to the guard. The system does not show the person in the operations center what the key number is. For every key request, there are two levels of security.

After an envelope is opened, the key must be returned to the Provident operations center. A new unique number is generated for the key and it is once again sealed in a manila envelope with a unique number on the outside. The envelope then must be returned to the original vehicle where it came from. At all times, the wallboards in the operations center indicate how many keys have been requested, are in use, and are awaiting recoding.

THRIVING WITH CHAOS

In the security business, all days, evenings, and nights are not created equal. Multiple alarms can be going off at the same time, each one clamoring for attention. If there is a natural event like a wind storm, activities in Provident's operations center can reach chaotic proportions due to the number of signals being received. In the past, employees found these events stressful and the risk of errors being made during these very busy times was high.

To bring order to the chaos and to deliver on their five-minute promise to customers, Mike identified key numbers that track the pulse of the business. His philosophy is to manage by exception. In Provident's operations center, all key indicators are displayed on large LCD monitors. All indicators are automatically updated in real time as events happen. Indicators are displayed in one of three colors:

Yellow: ....Good

Red: ....Coming up to deadline

Flashing Red:..Overdue

The more yellow, the calmer everything is. Mike says that even if there is an external event like a wind storm that causes alarms to go off all over the place, the color coding and the real time nature of the feedback keeps team members focused. In these moments of chaos, the operations center becomes the center for a military-style operation. Before these systems were in place a wind storm event could cause people to panic, hindering their responsiveness to the situation. The wallboards allow Provident employees to focus by making it clear which issues need to be prioritized.

CLARITY

For Mike, there were other benefits to introducing key productivity numbers. Everything is clearer to him and the employees. Mike no longer has to tell people what to do – his systems make it easy for employees to know what to do. Each person in the organization knows where they fit in the organization and there is less drama in their twenty-four hour operations. They now attach financial numbers to many of their key numbers, so that employees know whether this is a $60,000 impact or a $100 one. With the financial impact clearly attached to the KPI, revenue numbers grow faster.

There are systems in place at Provident to measure the quality of the work being done. When key numbers were first introduced the numbers went up, but at the expense of quality. New quality control measures needed to be introduced. Mike says that Provident employees want to do a great job. The key numbers let team members know how they are doing relative to one another. Peer pressure helps keep the numbers moving to perfection.

Every Provident employee "owns a number." Employee groups meet together in huddles for fifteen minutes every day to discuss the issues of the day. In these huddles, employees have to "own up" to what the real number is. This transparency makes it easier for people to take ownership of issues and ensures that employees have the data they need. Because feedback is in real time there is instant gratification—"do it well and the number improves."

KEEP IT SIMPLE

Mike believes that the clearest path to success is to keep things simple. Finding just a handful of KPIs that drive your business is tremendously hard work. The example of the keys shows how hard it is to keep it simple.

While customers think it should be simple to integrate and monitor all their systems, the truth is that it takes a highly skilled technician to install an alarm system that can be fully integrated with all the systems in a home or office. In new installations today, Provident integrates a minimum of three independent systems and often many more. Not only does Mike have to find these skilled technicians, they also monitor quality and billable versus non-billable installation hours.

The proliferation of cheaper monitoring technology combined with the simplicity of phone apps has changed the alarm company landscape. Provident Security makes it simple by appealing to people who want a live person who can respond in real-time to events as they happen whether this is to due to an intrusion alarm or a flood that has started while the customer is away on holidays. Mike's team are there within five minutes—guaranteed.

LESSONS LEARNED

Mike is a leader who has a passion for understanding and then meeting the greatest needs of his customers. He has developed his businesses to be a Promise Delivery System. Mike made the commitment to put people, process, systems, and accountability in place so that Provident can deliver on their promises—not just talk about them. Here are some key lessons from Mike's success:

1. Identify a key aspect of an industry that is underperforming.
2. Commit to a measurable brand promise.
3. Continually improve your people and processes to deliver on your brand promise.
4. Find and hire the right people who can ensure your organization will excel at fulfilling its brand promise.

The results have been spectacular. Provident is the fastest growing security company in Vancouver. And, Provident is still working on ways to innovate and get even better. Good is never good enough for them.

TAKE ACTION NOW

The highest performing businesses know how they are operating from moment to moment, not just at week, month, or quarter end. Every business operates on just a handful of critical measures. Companies at the top of their operational game look at critical customer interactions, making sure they deliver on a measurable brand promise. Move your operations to the next level with these actions:

1. Within 30 days, meet with your senior management team and pick one KPI to measure and report weekly to the team and the company on the one you picked.
2. In the next 7 days, measure the responsiveness to inbound leads from the telephone and your web site.

3. Before the month is out, call ten customers and ask them about their experience with your quality and support. Write down and share your findings with your team.

FINANCIAL STRATEGY

It was a sunny December day when we sailed from France to Spain for the first time. The wind was blowing hard from the right direction. We were sailing along, having a great day. The previous day I had plotted our route in the mapping software on our laptop. Because this was the first time we had ever done the route, I was being extra careful to monitor all systems, making sure we were where we were supposed to be.

The alarm on the depth sounder suddenly went off and said that the water was less than eight feet (two meters) deep. Since Dragonsinger drew just under eight feet, I was in a panic that we were about to hit the bottom. I turned the boat away from shore—I knew that was where deeper water lay. This put our boat sideways to the wind and waves. A large wave slapped the hull and as our ten-year-old son Kevin watched the wave ricocheted off the hull, into the air, where the wind took the spray and drenched him. Allen, our youngest child, was huddling under the dodger and was spared from getting hit by the waves. Years later, Allen loves to tell the story of how his six-year-old self watched as Dad panicked and his older brother got soaked.

I eventually figured out that when our depth sounder couldn't sense the bottom, it often showed a bogus reading of very shallow water. We were in the right spot. The water was deep. Dragonsinger was new to us and we were still getting used to all its quirks. Financial statements are like that. You use budgets to set your route, but then you have to constantly use real-time information to adjust against the budget you set. If you haven't done this much or you are turning the business in a new direction, it takes time to sift through the data.

You need a plan for your financial strategy. Not just budgets, but an overall capitalization and cash flow plan. Then, you need to constantly monitor financial performance against these plans.

IT'S NOT THE NUMBERS

At Robelle, Kerry Lathwell handled our monthly financial statements. My constant directive to her was:

> "It's not about the numbers. It's about what the numbers mean."

Just like our sailing story, you have to know when the numbers are really telling you that you are off course versus when they don't correctly represent the situation. Over time, I would ask Kerry questions about the financial statements she was producing and about what the different numbers mean. Eventually, Kerry would anticipate my questions, providing senior management with a summary of the critical information, what was on track, and, more importantly, what was not.

CASH FLOW

As a small business owner, cash is king. Run out of cash and you are probably out of business. Matching your accounts receivable to your accounts payable is one key factor to monitor. Many entrepreneurs start their week by looking at the cash balance in the bank, using this as a proxy for the health of their cash flow. Accrual accounting can often mask the real situation with cash.

Jim McFarlane is the founder and CEO of Explorer Construction Management Software, a global leader in providing ERP solutions to the construction industry in the UK, US, Canada, and Australia. Jim starts his day by looking at two pie charts in each region. One shows total receivables and one shows total payables. Jim has a ratio goal of approximately five times more receivables than payables. If each region is maintaining that ratio, Jim is happy. Jim has gone through past experiences where he has seen the ratio be reversed with payables being five times higher than receivables—these were not happy times for Jim.

WORKING CAPITAL

When planning your financial strategy, you will eventually need to have working capital. Not only will you need to fund the accounts payable/receivable spread, there is also inventory, payroll, commissions, and numerous other items that are paid out before you can collect the money for goods and services you have provided.

Strong cash flow management leads to lower needs of working capital. This is an area that needs to have someone keeping a constant eye on it. Whether or not you use Jim's KPI above, do check the cash balance every Monday, or devise some other system to monitor working capital. You want to be on top of your cash and working capital on a daily or at least weekly basis.

MANAGE RELATIONSHIPS

All business is about managing relationships. Everything related to the cash flow and financing of your business is also about relationships. If the only time you go to your bank is to ask for money, you will have no relationship with them. Banking fees, multi-currency accounts, maximizing exchange rates, and optimizing your banking transactions should all be part of a yearly review process with your key banking contact.

PROFIT IS NOT A FOUR-LETTER WORD

Are you focused on building a profitable company? You might be surprised at how many entrepreneurs start a company without thinking through this question. Just because you are passionate about solving a particularly painful problem for people who are willing to pay you money for the solution doesn't mean you will actually make money. I have met entrepreneurs who have told me:

"We were losing money on every transaction, but I knew that we could make it up on volume."

Such businesses do not last. Even worse, they often go through a lot of other people's money before finally crashing and burning. The truth is that

> Make sure that you are making a profit after taking a fair salary for your own contributions to the business.

your business should be making money. Once you are profitable you control your own destiny.

When looking at your profit, be sure you have taken an adequate salary before figuring your profits. Many entrepreneurs make sure that all of their employees and suppliers are paid, but then do not pay themselves a fair wage. My accountant explained it this way to me:

"Figure out what you would pay an independent third person to manage your business."

Making a lot of money is a yardstick that you are doing an excellent job of satisfying a market and being highly efficient at running your business. There is nothing to apologize for to anyone for making great money or for paying yourself a market salary.

If you are making money, you will need to decide what to do with those profits. Some of the common strategies for profits include:

1. Paying outside investors a dividend.

2. Reinvesting all or part of the profit into working capital and future growth (capital equipment, product development, people development, and more).

3. Taking most of the profit yourself and sharing the rest with your employees.

TAX PLANNING

In the 90s, Robelle was making money. In Canada at that time, the maximum marginal tax rate was over 50%. While I would have much preferred to put more time and energy into acquiring more customers and keeping them happy, taxes had such a big impact on how much of our profits we could keep that we spent a lot of time working out the best tax strategies.

This is an area where you need specialized advice. Taxation is incredibly complex, constantly changing, and even more challenging when dealing with multiple jurisdictions. There are a bewildering number of ways you can run your business from a tax point of view to maximize the deductions you can claim and the profit you can keep, either in the business or personally.

FUNDING YOUR DREAM

I've met numerous entrepreneurs who maxed out their credit cards starting their business. Others mortgage their homes. Every business has its own unique need for capital and you will have your own appetite for financial risk.

Mike Volker, one of Canada's best known angel investors, keeps a list of Money Links[9] with types of capital for your business: green, gold, and red. Green capital funds growth and includes investors who are willing to purchase stock in your business to fund your growth. Gold are funds from government or their agencies that include grants, tax credits, interest-free loans, and other incentives. These are unique to each country, state/province, and municipality where you operate, but can be golden in helping finance your business. Mike's final category is red, which includes all debt instruments.

Whether you agree with Mike's colors or not the important point is that money comes with different terms and conditions. Some entrepreneurs prefer to take on a manageable amount of debt rather than the burden of outside investors. Your location, business model, stage, and many other factors will improve or limit your chances of obtaining government money. Just be sure to consider the different forms of capital you can obtain for your business.

---

9   http://www.sfu.ca/%7Emvolker/biz/moneylnk.htm

Remember that preselling your product idea to the first few customers can be a great source of capital and market validation. Kickstarter can be used to raise funds to develop your product while validating that you actually have a product in the first place. Be as creative in finding capital as you are in every other part of your business.

MONEY IS A COMMODITY

I spent four years as an angel investor looking at over four hundred business plans, angel pitches, and business opportunities. In all of these pitches, I was just one angel investor among many.

> If you are looking for investors, find those with the time and talents to help grow your business.

Money is a commodity. A dollar is a dollar is a dollar. As we covered in the previous section, the terms and conditions attached to the money are at least as important as the money itself.

Beyond the money, look at the people who you will work with to obtain and manage capital. If you are seeking outside investors, the value of the time those investors bring to your business should far exceed the value of the money they are investing. For all sources of capital, look for people who bring expertise, knowledge, and contacts that can be useful to your business. You will need to take a lot of time to find whatever capital you are looking for. Use that time wisely to focus on the gaps you have in your business and how you can find the right people to help you fill those gaps. Use the chapters of this book as a guide to the ten strategic areas of your business and consider which ones need the most work as you seek outside financing.

PEOPLE, IDEA, AND MARKET

Outside investors look for three things in a business they are considering investing in: the people; the idea or competitive advantage the entrepreneur brings to the table; and the size, growth, and fit in the market of the idea being presented. Not only must you have 100% passion for what you are doing, your co-founders and senior management team must complement you and your idea.

If you have worked together as a successful team, let us know. If one of your team members has specialized knowledge, contacts, or market presence (e.g., they are the acknowledged thought leader in the field) leverage that to help outside investors create belief in you and your team.

SELL TO RAISE MONEY

Convincing a bureaucrat that they should give you money from a government program? You are selling. Meeting with bankers to arrange a line of credit? Selling again. Are you looking to sell stock to investors? More selling. All sources of outside capital require some kind of process to validate you and your company.

If you treat the process of raising money as a sales process while remembering that the people with the money have their own buying process, you will act

> When raising money of any kind remember to formulate the process from the point of view of the people with the money.

and respond appropriately. Find out what the norms are for the type of money you are looking for and then communicate and present in a way that is consistent with what the people with the money are expecting. They will appreciate you approaching them from their point of view and you will improve the chances that you get the capital you are seeking and the terms and conditions that will be attached to them. Remember that you are selling yourself and your idea—not your products.

BUSINESS PLAN

In *The Art of the Start*, Guy Kawasaki suggests that the traditional 96-page business plan is still useful, if only for you and your team to prove that you can work together to produce a plan. While there is a lot of truth in this, I believe in keeping it simple. Can you describe your business on the back of an envelope? In 30 seconds? Have you covered the ten strategies in this book or the ten points Kawasaki makes in his? Does your pro forma financial plan make sense? Do you have a short slide deck and four-page summary that captures the essence of what you are trying to do? Are you clear on your milestones, project plans, and use of the capital you want to raise?

Many funding sources will require one or more of these shorter documents in order to move ahead. In today's fast-paced world, fewer of us require and/or will even take the time to review a business plan longer than fifty pages. Be sure to know your market and whom you are trying to raise funds from so that you create the right documents for those you are selling to.

If you are investing your profits back into the business, it still makes sense for the senior management team to have a pro forma spread sheet with financial projections of revenue and expenses (optimistic, realistic, and pessimistic) plus a short two to four-page overview that summarizes all key aspects of a growth initiative. The summary, along with measureable milestone goals, is a great tool for helping to get alignment inside and outside the organization to get people on board and to stay on track as you move forward with your plans.

INCREMENTAL REVENUE IS NOT INCREMENTAL

Entrepreneurs come up with new ideas all the time. So do their employees. For new revenue opportunities, you need to think and act like an investor. Start with a back of the napkin income statement showing how you will make money with a new initiative. Follow that with a simple balance sheet showing how much capital you will need to invest in order to become profitable. It always takes more capital and more time than you think.

> New revenue opportunities all take more capital and time than you think. Allow for that in your planning.

We often talk ourselves into taking on a new product line or selling something new based on the idea that there is little incremental cost. There is always incremental cost. What is the cost of distracting your sales people on the new product line? Assume they only spend 25% of their time on the new product line; that means only 75% of their time is spent on your existing products and revenue projections.

You need to invoice and collect payments. Manage relationships with your suppliers. Keep your sales team motivated. Have support handle the new product line. Any new business should be treated as if you were starting a new business from scratch. You have the advantage of existing relationships, customers, infrastructure, employees, and processes. Use these to be successful while making sure you estimate the true revenue potential and costs. Then, measure the success of the new product line independently.

Case Study:
KEN SIMPSON, FOUNDER AND CEO, MAILCHANNELS

A pivotal life moment led Ken Simpson to decide that he only wanted to pursue his passions in life. He partnered with another young engineer to found MailChannels to tackle the problem of email spam. A decade and several financings later, they are gaining traction with some of the largest ISPs and telecom companies in the world.

BACKGROUND

After founding his first company in 2001, an early WiFi hotspot provider, Ken Simpson was looking for what to do next. While doing consulting work to pay the bills, he reconnected with an old university friend, Will Whittaker, meeting weekly with him during the summer of 2003 to brainstorm ideas for a new company. After a few meetings, Will presented a breakthrough idea for spam prevention using disposable email addresses.

Then, without warning, tragedy struck. A visit to the hospital's emergency department confirmed that Ken and Yvette had lost their first baby at 36 weeks, just a few short weeks away from full term. Ken and Yvette were devastated.

After a night in the hospital with Yvette, Ken got a phone call from his principal consulting client asking if he was coming in that day. In a moment of total clarity, Ken realized that he was never going back to his consulting job. He committed himself to only working on his own passions.

USING UP SAVINGS

After a month of mourning, Ken needed something to occupy his mind. Ken and Will put their energy full time towards MailChannels in the summer of 2004, but by the fall, money was starting to get tight. At one point, Ken advanced $12,000 on his Visa card, leaving him feeling like he was holding a ticking time bomb.

Luckily for Ken, an angel investor from his previous venture, Malcolm Collins, had taken an interest in MailChannels, agreeing to help him arrange a modest angel round. With Malcolm's help and connections, they closed a $100K round of convertible debt while securing some government grant money to help defray R&D costs.

FIRST PRODUCT

Ken and Will were both engineers. As Ken says, "We had no idea of what marketing and sales even were. No idea of cold calling, how to get customers, or how to support them." By now, Ken was learning that $100K doesn't go very far when you are paying four developers, need office space, and have to go to conferences. By the fall of 2005 MailChannels was running out of money. Even with the grant money, by October the team was being paid in stock. A key developer simply left one day, never to return.

While at a conference, Ken connected with a New York client that needed help with their email infrastructure. They took on the client on a consulting basis, giving the company critical cash flow, while buying Ken time to figure out the next steps for financing and building MailChannels.

A TIME OF CHANGE

In September, Ken made a bold decision and decided to abandon their first product and focus instead on a new product, Traffic Control, that could reuse much of the software the team had already written. Ken comments, "A potential customer had told us that our first idea sucked, but that if we could do this other thing, he'd be really interested. I was convinced—what else were we going to do?"

Ken then hired Jeff Omstead, an account executive who had sold anti-spam solutions in the first half of the decade. Jeff worked his Rolodex and by January 2006 had found MailChannels' first Traffic Control trial customer. While Ken and the team knew how to develop software, they had limited experience in deploying and scaling software. As Ken says "We destroyed our first trial customer's email systems for hours at a time." While the prospect was patient, eventually he couldn't take the outages and told Ken he was no longer interested.

Ken then hired Stas Beckman, who not only brought additional skills in software scalability, deployment, and field debugging, but a huge email list. Stas sent out an email request to his list, which resulted in MailChannels closing its first ever customer, Sunflower Broadband.

SECOND ROUND FINANCING

Ken had spent all of his personal savings, raised a $100K equity round, was starting to build a pipeline of potential customers, and was still running out of money. Based on their sales pipeline, Ken was able to raise his second round of equity financing. He presented to and met with many local angel investors and raised another $150K in the fall of 2006.

With this infusion of money, the team was able to sell to more customers. Their business model was to sell licenses on a yearly basis. As 2007 approached, these customers were starting to renew their original licenses, helping with their cash flow.

NEW DIRECTION

Based on their growing revenues and the potential of their market, Ken brought in an expert to craft a new investment presentation. While based in Vancouver, BC, Ken applied to the Seattle Alliance of Angels. "Seattle Alliance had a rigorous three-stage review process, which was fantastic for honing our pitch," remembers Ken. "And by the third stage, we had a couple of angels from their group who were already interested in leading a round." Based on the strength of Ken's vision, product, and market analysis, he was able to raise $250K from the Seattle angels and an additional $250K from his existing and new Vancouver angel investors.

With new investors came a new board of directors who were pushing hard to ramp up sales. They were telling Ken to spend the investment quickly in order to grow MailChannels as fast as possible. In the meantime, Jeff Omstead had hit a wall on the sales front, despite working 12-hour days and hitting the phones as hard as humanly possible. Where they had once been able to find new prospects, Jeff had maxed out his Rolodex and was coming up completely dry.

A DOWNTURN

With little success in 2007, disappointing the expectations of the new investors and directors, Ken felt tremendous pressure to market and sell faster. He hired more people, including a consultant who analyzed the market and concluded that the enterprise anti-spam market had matured and probably wasn't the best place to go looking for customers. The consultant advised that the ISP market was still facing major email challenges, and if MailChannels was going to survive, it should probably start talking to ISPs.

While they closed one ISP customer with a five-digit deal, the pipeline was very small when the financial crisis began in the fall of 2008. Ken actively participated in a monthly CEO peer group. Ken and his peers realized that what VCs like Kleiner Perkins were saying was true. Only those that cut immediately and cut deeply would survive to win another day. Ken slowed down and dedicated himself to learning more about sales and marketing. He realized that his weakness in this area could doom the company he started.

It was a dark time for Ken. He was ready to give up. What kept him going was his fear of being unemployed. "To be honest, the fear of unemployment was once again the thing that kept me going," admits Ken. To Ken's credit, he also felt an obligation to one day give something back to all the investors who had believed in him over the years.

ANOTHER NEW PRODUCT

By 2009, MailChannels had identified that outbound email spam was a tremendous problem for global ISPs and telecom providers. They even had a Thai mobile operator who was willing to be a beta customer for the new outbound product. Unfortunately, like Traffic Control, the first version wasn't ready for prime time. The server that was processing all of the email coming out of the entire network crashed, leaving a million people without email for many hours. The Thai company stopped returning calls after that.

Getting desperate, Ken had a breakthrough moment. He led an invitation-only anti-spam conference in Vancouver and asked some of the biggest players in the world to attend. Spam was still a huge challenge for everyone, but especially large ISPs and telecom companies. The anti-spam "Czar" at Yahoo came to the conference and shared on the techniques Yahoo was using to fight spam. Yahoo realized the community benefit of putting their cards on the table and appealing to the top experts in the world to all raise their game to excel at killing off spam.

This event cemented MailChannels' leadership and commitment to focusing exclusively on their new Outbound Anti-Spam product line. They successfully applied for and won a rigorous RFP process for one of the largest telecom companies in the world.

MANAGING THE CASH

By the fall of 2011, MailChannels was out of money. Even though some early enterprise customers were still renewing, the revenue wasn't generating a profit, even with a team of three. Sales of the new outbound anti-spam product were extremely infrequent, as the company hadn't yet been able to afford any kind of marketing or sales effort to boost its prospects.

There were many times when Ken had to gauge whether he could meet the next payroll. More times than he cares to remember, he literally did not know where the money would come from, yet every time he somehow found a way to get it done. While the global telecom deal was six digits in size, collecting the money was a long and drawn out process. Ken created a debt instrument with a relatively high interest rate that existing investors bought into, so that Ken could manage through lengthy accounts receivable timelines.

Realizing that he had no chance to raise another round of financing, Ken finally took sales and marketing seriously. He spent even more time figuring out the market, carefully recruited, hired, and managed a new sales person, and took personal ownership of marketing and sales. The results were spectacular, with revenues doubling in 2013.

For the legacy Traffic Control customers, Ken went to monthly instead of yearly subscriptions. This proved to be easier to sell, easier to collect, and smoothed out the bumps in cash flow they were used to experiencing. Ken also found that they could charge more on a monthly basis. His increasing focus on marketing and sales has resulted in increased revenue, better cash flow, and fewer worries about meeting payroll.

LESSONS LEARNED

It took Ken a decade, but he has found a sweet spot in the market where his company can make a difference in the battle against spam. The lessons he learned along the way include:

1. A CEO has to learn marketing and sales, including market needs and how to manage sales people and the sales process.
2. It takes tremendous tenacity to continue financing and building a business.
3. A peer group of CEOs has been a key factor in Ken being able to continue.
4. A change in business model, from yearly to monthly subscription fees, had a disproportionate impact on MailChannels' cash flow.
5. It's no fun being almost out of cash. Believe in yourself and what you have created, finding creative ways to manage your cash and keep going.

We are all inundated with spam every day, which experts estimate comprises over 75% of all email. Thankfully, there are people like Ken Simpson and MailChannels who fight the battle every day to remove spam from our email environment.

TAKE ACTION NOW

The most valuable companies in the world know how to make money. They also know that financial statements are just a tool to help them deeply understand how their business is operating and how they can improve both their top and bottom-line revenue. Financial planning means not just understanding your cash flow, but how much capital is needed to generate that cash flow. Great businesses know where they are all the time. Know where you are financially by:

1. Measuring your cash every Monday morning and tracking how it changes over time.

2. Identifying one key number that can be derived from your financial statements to drive your growth within this quarter.

3. In your next yearly plan, have agreement from all senior management team on the exact amount of financing you need to fuel your next year of growth.

EXIT STRATEGY

After twenty years at Robelle, I had just sold my stake in the company to Bob Green, the original founder. It was early 2001 and as I cast around for what was next for me I hadn't even noticed that the dot com meltdown was happening.

I utilized my network looking for opportunities. About a month later, I was referred to Margaret Livingston, who had her own business helping place people who had been let go from their positions. We had lunch together. Afterwards, we returned to her office and while we were sitting together Margaret made a pivotal statement that was to change my life:

"David, your kids will never be 11, 9, and 5 again."

I had never really thought about an exit strategy. I likely thought I was going to be with Robelle forever, even though as a technology company, the business was unlikely to last forever. When Margaret made that statement to me it was like the proverbial light bulb came on in my head.

That conversation opened up possibilities. Karalee and I discussed it and decided to commission a boat in the Mediterranean, move on board, and home school our three children, Jocelyn, Kevin, and Allen. In true entrepreneurial fashion, we planned for one year, but once we got out there our plans actually took two years. That time changed our lives forever. Karalee and I now have a family legacy that we draw on every day.

You do not have to wait until the last minute to have an exit strategy. In fact, the best exit strategies start at the beginning.

START WITH THE END IN MIND

Bob, Annabelle, and I created our first company together around 1986. It was an R&D company that was contracted by the main company to do all development work. This helped us build discipline in our product planning and development, while making it easier for us to claim Canada's software, research, and development (SR&ED) tax credits.

As part of starting the R&D company we created a shareholders agreement. I hired a lawyer to review the agreement with me. The agreement included a shotgun clause. In a typical shotgun clause, one shareholder can make an offer to the other shareholders. Under the terms of the clause, the other shareholders either sell all of their shares to the person making the offer or they turn around and buy all the shares of the person making the offer at the price being offered. While an all-or-nothing approach (and thus the name shotgun clause), it does provide for an exit strategy. At the time, I recall asking my lawyer why such a clause was needed. After all, I said that I would never get to a point of not getting along with Bob and Annabelle.

Fortunately, the lawyer I hired was older and smarter than I. The shotgun clause was kept intact through several different corporate organizations and shareholders agreements. In 2001, Bob Green and I had a fundamental difference in the strategic direction of Robelle. Both strategies were viable, but they were not complimentary. The shotgun clause was the way that I was able to exit Robelle.

Whether you have a shotgun clause or not, having an exit strategy, even one far into the future, helps to protect you and the company. If you ever plan to sell your company, starting with the end in mind maximizes the value you will get.

INVESTOR EXPECTATIONS

If you bring in outside investors, they will have expectations about your company. These might be that you make a profit and they share in a percentage of that profit. More likely, they will be looking for you to make

> You are one of the biggest investors in your company. Make sure that you set your own expectations as an investor.

an exit valued many times greater than what they invested in the company.

For example, angel investors typically expect to see a return ten times their initial investment within five years of making the investment. If you attracted this type of investment, it is likely that you showed your angel investors a possible exit plan when you asked them to invest. Like all plans, this will have changed as your company and your markets changed. Make sure you keep your investors informed of your changing exit strategy as conditions change.

Even if you have no outside investors, you, and any partners you have, are the single biggest investors in your own company. Treat your company as an investment. What do you get out of the business? Make sure that you consider your financial goals and what you and any partners get out of the business on a non-financial basis (e.g., fulfilling your purpose which we discussed in Corporate Strategy).

TIMELINES

While you should always have a general exit strategy in mind, a realistic timeline for a specific exit plan is three years. More than that and conditions are likely to change too much. At a minimum you will need at least a year to put together all the key information, build a marketing plan, and then start the process of actively attracting buyers for your business.

CREATE BELIEF TO SELL

Selling your entire business requires that you create belief in your team, markets, products, and your ability to consistently deliver on your revenue and profit goals as laid out in the plans you create. As a business owner, you may be required to stay on for one or

> Buyers want to know that your business can deliver revenue and profit to plan without you being there.

two years. Buyers will be looking to see how your team can operate with someone else leading them.

STRATEGIC BUYERS

There are many reasons for buying a business. Strategic buyers will pay more for your business than someone who just wants to add another business to their portfolio to generate profits. Look for buyers who operate in your markets, but who have a gap in the product offering you fill or buyers who are looking for customers like the ones you have attracted. Understanding the goals of your buyers, even if you can only guess at them, is important to positioning your company to maximize your exit price.

Competitors can make great strategic buyers. If your corporate culture has many of your employees viewing competitors as "the enemy", there are practical considerations during and after closing a sale to a competitor. You want to ensure that your employees are motivated to continue performing at historic levels so that you can prove their ability to continue producing the results in your business plan. After the sale, you need to demonstrate to employees why it is in their best interests to work with the new management team.

BUSINESS PLAN

While you may have operated your business without a business plan in the past, you will need a business plan in order to sell your business. This plan should go back one year with actual financial numbers and project forward three years. Buyers will be looking to make sure that during the sales and due diligence process, you continue to deliver the results in your business plan.

It will take input from your entire management team to create a complete business plan. This includes your corporate history, your markets, how you position your business and your products in these markets, the outside validation of your market growth numbers, bios of key executives, your key productivity indicators and how you measure them, along with pro forma financial statements.

Buyers will believe you more if you have audited financial statements. Unaudited statements leave too many opportunities for the numbers to be fudged. One reason to plan an exit three years in advance is to start the process of auditing your financial statements, so that once you are into the exit process you can show prospective purchasers three years of audited results.

DATA VAULT

All prospective buyers will have a due diligence process. Before that starts, you will need to provide critical documents to prospective buyers. These should include:

> Create a data vault of critical documents buyers need in order to do their diligence.

- Your business plan
- Audited financial statements for at least the prior year
- A digital copy of the minute book
- Copies of critical employee, intellectual property, vendor, and partner contracts

To keep the process fair and to ensure that you keep control of when and who accesses these documents, set up a digital secure data vault with all of these documents. Use care when using third-party services as they have their own terms and conditions that may not meet the security requirements of you or your potential buyers.

HIRING TO SELL

Selling a business is a specialized process. There are individuals and firms that do nothing but specialize in selling businesses as part of mergers and acquisitions. Look for the following when hiring someone to sell your business:

1. Expertise in positioning and selling businesses.
2. A track record of high valuations.
3. Ability to bring more than one buyer to the table.

4. Proven bidding processes to maximize value from multiple bidders.

5. References from other entrepreneurs who have worked with them.

You should be cautious with who you get to sell your business. If you want to do it yourself, make sure you have the skills and the time to sell your business. Remember that if things go really well, the entire process will take a year.

There are no norms for fees for selling a business. Most firms and individuals charge a retainer and a percentage of the sale price. The specifics vary widely. For details on fees, see the blog post M&A Advisor Fees for Selling a Business[10] by Basil Peters (author of *Early Exits*).

LIMITATIONS OF THE ENTREPRENEUR

When buying a business, buyers pay more for a business that can create a plan and then operate the business according to that plan. It is exceedingly difficult for an entrepreneur to be present to ensure that the business is operating at peak efficiency, while at the same time marketing, positioning, and selling the business. At a minimum you will be spending half your time for one year to complete a successful exit.

As the entrepreneur, it is challenging to have an unemotional bias to the business and what it is worth. Your blood, sweat, and tears have gone into building your business. Potential buyers are going to bring problems and concerns forward—often as an intentional effort to reduce the purchase price. It is critical that you do not react emotionally when buyers start calling your business ugly. Better to have a board member or third-party handle the sale from an independent viewpoint.

LEAVING IT TOO LATE

Many entrepreneurs are so wrapped up in their business that they never take the time to think about their exit strategy until it is too late. Markets change and what once might have been a hugely profitable market has

10   http://www.exits.com/blog/ma-advisor-fees-selling-business/

now turned into a cutthroat commodity market where no one makes money. If you decide to sell at this point, you will get a fraction of what you might have obtained at the peak of the potential for your business.

> Timing is critical for a successful exit. Start planning for it from the beginning. Leave it too late and you may have nothing to exit with.

I am always saddened when I attend a family business event or a session on selling your business when I see an older couple long past the age of retirement that listen in bewilderment about the challenges of selling their business. These entrepreneurs are often reaching the end of their life and still have not thought about an exit strategy. While they might have once hoped that one of their children would take over the business, that day has long passed. I only hope that they take action to sell their business before their estate has to do it for them. By then, the business may not even be worth anything.

KEEPING THE REWARDS

It is harder to keep the money from your business than it was to get it in the first place. As an entrepreneur, you are used to taking risks. Having successfully sold your business, it is time to keep the rewards—not take a lot of new risk with it.

If you want to invest in a new business, only take a small portion, say 3% of your net worth, to invest in high risk ventures like a new business. Hire a professional investment advisor who can provide perspective on what you are doing with your capital, including the risk of the decisions you are making about what to do with the result of all your hard work. As an early advisor once told me:

> *"It's much harder to keep your money than it was to earn it in the first place."*

Case Study:
GEOF AUCHINLECK, CO-FOUNDER NEOTERIC

Two founders live eight time zones apart and use the separation to build a successful technology business in healthcare. After working on their business for 10 years, they leverage their commercial success in the United Kingdom to expand in the US. Maintaining clear communication about their exit strategy, despite their separation, allows them to be ready to sell when the opportunity comes. Almost.

BACKGROUND

In 1997, both Geof Auchinleck and Lyn Sharman saw a need for more automation in healthcare. They had worked together at MDS, a company that pioneered the automation of laboratory sample handling. Corporate changes forced Lyn and Geof to leave MDS and start out on their own. Luckily, they were equipped with plenty of ideas on how to improve service delivery in hospitals.

Within months of founding Neoteric in Vancouver, British Columbia, Lyn's personal situation changed and he moved to England. For many, this could have put an end to their fledgling company, but for Neoteric this led naturally to their first sales successes.

CRITICAL MEETING

Geof was the product manager and developer, while Lyn was the sales guy in the partnership. With Lyn based in the UK, they started visiting hospitals there. They had a seminal meeting with the lab manager at a Manchester Hospital where they were pitching their initial product idea. They quickly sensed that their product idea wasn't going anywhere and asked the lab manager what was the biggest problem he was facing.

The lab manager looked at a nearby refrigerator and said, "that's my problem." The fridge held blood. While there was a logbook in which every addition or removal of blood units from the fridge was to be recorded it was never accurate. The lab manager never knew for sure where the blood had gone. He challenged Geof and Lyn, asking "Can you do something about managing the blood in my refrigerator?"

A PRODUCT IS BORN

Geof was so inspired he designed the prototype of their product on the plane ride back to Canada. He had noticed that every blood unit utilized technology from the 1970s—a barcode. Geof's breakthrough moment was the thought that if patients had a barcode on their wrist band, it would be simple to scan the barcode on both the blood units and the patient, ensuring a correct match.

Blood matching before operations requires a huge amount of time and great expense, to say nothing of the risk it poses to patients. Before Neoteric, hospital staff had to look at each operation for the day then plan for a worst case scenario of 1-4 units of blood for each of these operations. In many cases, there was little or no need for blood in an operation, meaning a tremendous amount of effort was wasted preparing and stocking blood products.

By using Neoteric's technology, hospitals could move to just-in-time blood delivery. Because they could accurately track what blood they had on hand and quickly, even in the middle of an operation, obtain the right blood unit for a patient, the entire planning and overbooking of blood resources was eliminated at hospitals that deployed Neoteric technology.

BUILDING ON SUCCESS

There were many iterations of their product line. Because Lyn was based in the middle of England it was possible for him to visit almost any hospital in the UK within a single day's drive. This made it possible for Neoteric to have massive success and gain deep penetration into the UK healthcare market.

The struggle occurred when they decided to expand into the US. While they had five successful American installs, they realized that it would take a serious marketing and sales effort to penetrate the US market. Building a direct sales force from scratch would take too many people and a long time, so Geof and Lyn decided to look for a partner based in the US.

They settled on Mediware, a Kansas-based company that already sold transfusion management software to the US healthcare market. Neoteric's product was a logical extension of what Mediware already did. Mediware agreed to a non-exclusive contract for the US and Canada, with the stipulation that Neoteric could not deal with one of their competitors, who we will refer to as X Company.

ENTER HAEMONETICS

The Mediware partnership was rolling along, creating success, but not the same level of success that Neoteric had experienced in the UK. Geof and Lyn continued to look for other partners and had arranged a meeting with Haemonetics, "The Blood Management Company." When they entered the Haemonetics headquarters for their first meeting, there was a diagram on the wall of everything in the value-chain that Haemonetics did for blood management. There was a big hole in the middle of the diagram exactly where Neoteric would fit.

Geof was pumped as he entered the boardroom to present to the entire C-suite of Haemonetics. As part of their presentation, Geof presented an ROI calculator for Neoteric's product line. Their ROI calculator was based on a unit of blood costing hospitals $500 each, resulting in an average savings of $1M/hospital/year. The Chief Medical Officer of Haemonetics chimed in with the comment "you guys have it all wrong; a blood unit costs about $1,000."

With comments like that, Geof and Lyn thought signing Haemonetics as a distributor would be no problem; however, the CEO of Haemonetics soon told them that "we never distribute other people's products." Geof and Lyn were crestfallen, until the CEO said "we do purchase other companies." Geof and Lyn had no intention of positioning Neoteric that way, but wisely kept quiet and let the conversation proceed.

PLANNING AN EXIT

Even though Lyn lived in Warwick, England and Geof lived in Vancouver, BC, they got together on a regular basis to discuss the business and their lives. They made sure those discussions included what each of them wanted an exit to look like and a valuation that they each could live with. When Haemonetics was prepared to purchase Neoteric, they had a price in mind and were ready to sell when Haemonetics made an offer over their minimum.

While they were prepared to sell, the process was still a long and arduous one. To confirm that Haemonetics' offer was fair, Geof and Lyn hired an investment banker to offer Neoteric to the market. Their thinking was that the only way they could be sure they were getting a good price from Haemonetics was to bring another strategic buyer to the table.

After taking Neoteric to the market, the only other possible buyer to appear was X Company. Part of the distribution agreement Geof and Lyn had signed with Mediware included a no-sale clause to X Company. While Geof was on holidays with his family on a kayaking trip in Vancouver Island's Broken Group, he was also negotiating with Mediware to remove the no-sale clause from their contract. Not only did Geof have to give up family time, he learned that as part of their original contract they should have included specific language for change of control that would have made clauses like the non-compete one null and void.

WISE CHOICES

The financial meltdown of 2008 occurred as all this was happening. The offer on the table from X Company was cut to one-third of what they had previously offered. It was with trepidation that Geof called the CFO of Haemonetics to ask about the status of their offer. The response surprised Geof and taught him a valuable lesson.

The CFO responded that they hedge against big market swings. They had a budget and their offer was their offer—it wasn't changing due to the market changes. His one stipulation was that the deal absolutely must be completed prior to their next year-end on March 27, 2009.

Geof realized that when selling your company the quality of the people you are working with is far more important than the offer itself. People with high integrity will work through issues, be fair, and look after everyone involved in the transaction.

STEPS ALONG THE WAY

Geof and Lyn received professional and entrepreneurial advice through the entire development of Neoteric. Even with this help, they discovered that during one of their early financings, they were missing the signature of one of their angel investors on a critical document. The sale to Haemonetics could not go ahead without this signature.

Unfortunately, the investor had passed away in the intervening years. The executor of the estate had to be tracked down, the situation explained, and eventually the necessary signature was obtained. It would have been so much easier if the paperwork had been completed correctly in the first place a decade earlier.

THE DEAL IS OFF

Selling a company is a long, tedious, error-prone process filled with challenges. As part of the sales process, Neoteric had created a virtual data room containing all the critical documents. While Haemonetics had access to the data room from the very beginning, on the day of closing, they brought forward an issue with three patents they thought Neoteric could possibly be infringing on. Geof knew about these patents and had reviewed them to make sure Neoteric was not infringing but Haemonetics was not willing to take this risk. They insisted on an indemnity from Geof and Lyn that the two of them would be liable should there be any action involving these patents.

The clock was ticking on the absolute deadline given to Neoteric by the CFO of Haemonetics. Lyn was already in the Rose and Crown pub in Warwick, England prepared to hear that the funds had been wired to the shareholders. Geof had to scramble to contact Lyn to get back to the UK office to sign the indemnification document so that the deal could still close.

IT REALLY IS THE PEOPLE

With a heavy heart, Geof took a phone call from the CFO of Haemonetics just after the deadline. His opening comment to Geof was "We didn't wire the money to you." What the CFO said next demonstrated his integrity "I can't do this to you. The deadline was one I made and one that I can change. It is unfair to Lyn and you to hold you hostage on the patent issue. I will go to the board, explain the situation, and we will figure out how to close this fairly."

The CFO kept his word. The patent issue was figured out, and two weeks later the sale of Neoteric to Haemonetics closed. Geof and Lyn were convinced that they sold to the right people. Haemonetics lived up to their commitments. They kept the people—Lyn still works for them today. The product continued to evolve and eventually was fully integrated into Haemonetics' broader product offerings. The product continues to be a success today.

LESSONS LEARNED

The exit of Geof and Lyn as the founders and principal shareholders of Neoteric highlight many of the topics we have covered in this chapter:

1. Plan your exit from the start. As partners, you need to stay in touch and be in agreement about what an acceptable exit is.

2. When selling the company you have built, look beyond the surface to the quality and integrity of the company and the people you are selling to.

3. All corporate activities and intellectual property must be documented and a proper minute book kept up to date.

4. Use a virtual data room to gather together all key documents that will be needed by prospective acquirers.

The story of Neoteric is an inspiration. Not only did Geof and Lyn create a company and a product that makes hospitals safer for all of us, they looked after their employees and their product in addition to themselves before, during, and after the sale of Neoteric.

TAKE ACTION NOW

Throughout this book we state that successful entrepreneurs start with the end in mind and work backwards from there. Having a clear exit strategy keeps all of your other goals in alignment. When it comes time to sell your company, having all your critical documents to show prospective buyers can be the difference between success and failure. Potential strategic buyers can offer benefits other than being potential acquirers, so make sure you know who they might be. Be ready for your exit:

1. Meet with your senior management team in the next week and identify three strategic buyers you could sell the business to today.

2. Within a month, make sure that a senior member of your team meets with your lawyers and verifies that the minute book is up to date.

3. Before the quarter finishes, meet with your key financial stakeholders and define when you will exit and for how much.

GROW NOW

Accelerate and grow your business now. Do this by:

1. Getting out of the business to strategically focus on it.
2. Creating a new strategic plan and putting it into action.
3. Adjusting your course as you gain real-time feedback on the plan you put in action.

The entrepreneurs in this book demonstrate how changes in their thinking, combined with new ways of doing things created amazing results. Let their examples be an inspiration for you to take steps to raise your game to the next level.

YOU MAKE THE DIFFERENCE

You, the entrepreneur, are the single biggest impediment and advantage to the future of your business and your life. How you show up, your habits, and the way you interact with people have a disproportionate impact. The decisions you make about how you live your life will not only impact you, but your spouse, family, business partners, employees, and friends. Use the entrepreneurial examples in this book to show you how to be the best you can be.

SLOW DOWN TO SPEED UP

As entrepreneurs, we can get caught up in the adrenaline rush of the next crisis, decision, fire, or shiny red ball. It takes an act of courage to step away from the action to really figure out what it is you want. The very action of slowing down to think and plan is what will accelerate your success. As humans, we overestimate by a large margin what we can accomplish in a month or quarter, and underestimate what is possible in a year or three if we stay focused.

TAKE THE NEXT STEP

The choice is now up to you. You can continue to operate your business and your life the way you always have. This will guarantee that you will continue to get the results you always have. If you want different results, you have to take different action. All you need is one tiny step in a new direction. Take that step and accelerate your business in the next 90 days.

What Are You Waiting For?

ABOUT THE AUTHOR

While still in university getting his degree in computer science, David joined Robelle Solutions Technology as the first employee after the founders. After joining Robelle, he got permission from his 4th year professors to take a week off so he could fly to an international conference to give his first ever technical presentation.

During David's tenure as co-owner and President of Robelle, he traveled the world giving a new presentation every year, building Robelle into the world's leading provider of HP 3000 solutions. He is a co-author of The IMAGE/3000 Handbook, the reference work for the HP 3000 IMAGE database management system.

David has continued to dedicate his career to simplifying and explaining technical and management concepts to government and commercial organizations, their employees, and key stakeholders. Since leaving Robelle in 2001, he has been an investor, consultant and employee to a number of technology companies, focusing on turning ideas into products, messaging and results. David now works directly with entrepreneurs to help them bridge to the next level of results—in business and in life.

In his spare time, David enjoys the beauty, water, and mountains of the Vancouver area, while taking occasional adventure breaks with his wife, Karalee. David and Karalee are committed to their three children, spending time supporting them in the many and varied activities they are involved with, including skiing together as a family in Whistler.

When not writing books, coaching, or speaking, you might find David hiking the Himalayan Mountains of Nepal or sailing across oceans.

ADDITIONAL READING

Many authors have influenced my strategic thinking about business. Use this list for additional ideas on how to plan and operate your business.

- Achor, Shawn. *The Happiness Advantage: The Seven Principles of Positive Psychology That Fuel Success and Performance at Work.* Crown Business, 1st edition, 2010

- Collins, Jim. *Good to Great: Why Some Companies Make the Leap...And Others Don't.* Harper Business, 1st edition, 2001.

- Collins, Jim. *Built to Last: Successful Habits of Visionary Companies.* Harper Business, 1st edition, 2002.

- Edmonds, Chris. *The Culture Engine: A Framework for Driving Results, Inspiring Your Employees, and Transforming Your Workplace.* Wiley, 2014.

- Kawasaki, Guy. *The Art of the Start: The Time-Tested, Battle-Hardened Guide for Anyone Starting Anything.* Portfolio Hardcover, 1st edition, 2004.

- Moore, Geoffrey. *Crossing the Chasm, 3rd Edition: Marketing and Selling Disruptive Products to Mainstream Customers.* Harper Business, 3rd edition, 2014.

- Peters, Basil. *Early Exits: Exit Strategies for Entrepreneurs and Angel Investors (But Maybe Not Venture Capitalists).* MeteorBytes Data Management Corp, 1st edition, 2009.

- Smith, Guy. *Start-up CEO's Marketing Manual.* Free Thinkers Media, 2012.

INDEX

C

D

E

F

J

K

N

O

P

Q

R

S